PRAISE FOR **MAD MONK MANIFESTO**

"Monk Yun Rou's new book, *Mad Monk Manifesto*, is a Taoist call-to-action to anyone wishing to save themselves and the planet."

—Danielle Bolelli, PhD, author, professor, and host of
History on Fire and Drunken Taoist podcasts

"In this wide-ranging, amusing, and thoughtful book, *Mad Monk Manifesto: A Prescription for Evolution, Revolution, and Global Awakening*, Taoist Monk Yun Rou offers us a vision that can give hope to millions. It is a vision which is rooted in compassion, simplicity, and selflessness, and offers a pathway to a sustainable world—not just spiritually, but practically too. It is a book for snacking, but devouring too."

—Graeme Maxton, Secretary General of the Club of Rome
and author of bestselling books
The End of Progress and *Reinventing Prosperity*

"With *Mad Monk Manifesto*, Monk Yun Rou presents a utopian treatise that reminds us of what we can aspire to. He has much wisdom to share."

—Dr. Carl Pilcher, PhD, Blue Marble Space Institute of
Science, NASA (retired)

"Uplifting, inquisitive, and elegant in its delivery, Monk Yun Rou's newest work *Mad Monk Manifesto* shines a light on the importance of curiosity, kindness, and transformation in a world beset by overconsumption, the glorification of violence, and the relentless inundation and demands of the Information Age. A wonderful read for anyone looking to gain perspective and insight on the power of simplification and wonder!"

—Sarah Fimm, American singer-songwriter residing in Woodstock, NY

MAD MONK MANIFESTO

A Prescription for Evolution,
Revolution, and Global Awakening

ALSO BY YUN ROU
Yin: A Love Story

MAD MONK MANIFESTO

A Prescription for Evolution, Revolution, and Global Awakening

MONK YUN ROU

Mango Publishing
CORAL GABLES

For permission requests, please contact the publisher at:
Mango Publishing Group
2850 Douglas Road, 3rd Floor
Coral Gables, FL 33134 USA
info@mango.bz

For special orders, quantity sales, course adoptions and corporate sales, please
email the publisher at sales@mango.bz. For trade and wholesale sales, please
contact Ingram Publisher Services at customer.service@ingramcontent.com or
+1.800.509.4887.

Mad Monk Manifesto: A Prescription for Evolution, Revolution, and
Global Awakening

Library of Congress Cataloging-in-Publication number: 2018957576
ISBN: (print) 978-1-63353-864-1, (ebook) 978-1-63353-865-8
BISAC category code: PHI023000—PHILOSOPHY / Taoist

Printed in the United States of America

For Tasman Rosenfeld, who will most certainly make our world a better place.

CONTENTS

INTRODUCTION

You hold in your hands a manifesto for change, an eleventh-hour emergency survival manual utterly devoid of bright-future reassurances and New Age pabulum. You will find nothing here about how thinking positive thoughts will help you look great in tight jeans, how brilliant your children are, how the whales really love us for killing them, or how the work you do in your high-salaried corporate position is critical to the survival of the universe. Although I hope you will find my words as spiritual as they are political, I am no Pollyanna. I don't believe that all will soon be right with the world or that we are almost through the tough times. I don't accept social media as a substitute for reality, or that our evolving into half-digital cyborgs will take away all our pain. I believe in the transformative power of both meditation and love, but don't believe either or both will solve all our problems. I am a monk, not a carnival barker, and thus skeptical of quick and easy fixes; thus, I hope you will find the ones I offer in the chapters that follow to be substantial, meaningful, and worthwhile even though they may require effort. When contemplating these changes, please remember that change is the only constant our world offers.

I begin with such straightforward urgency because our floating home, zooming through the galaxy at high velocity inside the wildly spiraling solar system that contains it, has become a watery blue purgatory. More slaughterhouse than paradise, more frenzied, violent battlefield than garden of enlightenment, more cesspool of fractiousness than temple to unity, our beautiful planet is dying and we are its murderers. Wonders remain, but the effects of global industrialization, executed upon a foundation of Western values, guarantee such wonders won't last long. The values I refer to are mostly about what it means to be human, but also our greed, material excesses, species-centrism, the religiously-based notion of human hegemony over the natural world, and, of course, overpopulation.

The last item on that list may be obvious to those suffering traffic jams, polluted parks, and the disappearance of peace and quiet, but its global consequences are actually complex, underestimated, and inaccurately predicted. Wars over land, air, and water have already begun. The macro-organism we call Planet Earth, desperate to survive in its current, diverse glory, uses various methods to fight its way out from beneath the meaty weight of the human herd. These weapons include diseases, wars, automobile accidents, gender variances, and religious fundamentalism—anything and everything that pares down our numbers. Even so, there are still those who believe that their god encourages them to have ten children or more.

And then there is climate change, another feature of our greed, lack of sensitivity, and the religiously fundamentalist notion that the planet is our playground. Regardless of how many political leaders label it a hoax, weather patterns are changing at human, not geological, speed. It's tough to wrap our minds around the size of the changes and how soon they will be here. I write this as a displaced victim of one of the largest Atlantic hurricanes on record, having just watched the state of Texas suffer a thousand-year flood, and now seeing the state of California battling the largest and most deadly wildfire outbreak in recorded history. Tropical cyclones are growing more violent and frequent, ice caps are melting, glaciers and permafrost are disappearing, island nations are in existential peril. Tens of thousands of miles of coastline will soon be lost to oceans which are acidifying so rapidly that jellyfish will be the only "seafood" they can soon support. Vast continental plains are becoming deserts while deserts are becoming dustbowls, putting our food supply in jeopardy. Deforestation and marine algae die-offs suggest that the oxygen we breathe will eventually vanish. If all these challenges appeared in an apocalyptic Hollywood thriller, the screenwriter would be told to tone things down so as to make them believable.

Consider, too, the Sixth Great Extinction. The history of the earth—billions of years long, not the mere thousands of biblical fantasies—has seen five previous events of this type, variously caused by bursts of gamma-ray radiation from space, erupting volcanoes, and even the impact of asteroids. This latest extinction, though, is on us—the direct result of our activities and unchecked propagation. Who would have thought that humans could be so catastrophically destructive? Perhaps our atomic atrocities might have offered a clue. Any way you look at it, Earth is a bad place to be a non-human animal these days, be it an insect (whose indispensable group is severely affected), salamander, rhino, butterfly, tiger, turtle, or shark. The level of loss, thanks to our pesticides, condos, golf courses, cities, ocean trawling, and oh-so-much-more, is so staggering that scientists can't even fully assess it. Bottom line? We will never regain the natural world of our parents, and if our kids manage to survive over the long term, we wouldn't recognize the world they will inherit from us.

Thanks to the metastatic spread of certain Western values across the world, the nightmare we are facing is not just environmental, though without a habitable planet all other problems are obviously moot. Such foibles include violence, cruelty, greed, religious fundamentalism, and materialism, the last of which exists in inverse proportion to morality. It is time to educate against indulging bad behavior. It is time to see the sometimes-luscious literature of Abrahamic faiths within their original context and to bring their instructions and exhortations into the modern world. It is time to move beyond for-profit education offered on the basis of racially biased tests, the outrage of billionaires and yachts existing alongside homelessness and starvation, and the pernicious fiction that healthcare is a privilege and not as basic a right as any other afforded by civilized society. Failure to do so means the litany of human moral transitions will continue to poison the Western world and the Eastern world, too.

Despite our truly marvelous potential and episodic bursts of transcendent creativity, selflessness, heroism, and redemption, the violent ape known as *Homo sapiens* has proven thus far to be neither knowing nor wise. A fully fleshed-out catalog of our transgressions could fill the rest of this book and a hundred more, but, especially at this late hour in human history, I am more interested in a prescription than I am in a post-mortem. The prescription I offer involves a paradigm shift. We must abandon the Abrahamic faiths in their literal form. We must abandon the pernicious cycle that produces more technology, which in term creates apocalyptic problems, then create new technology to solve *those* problems, and on and on. This fruitless recipe, promulgated by material greed, does nothing but misdirect our attention away from the real problem, which is not so much what we do as who we are. We must stop relying on technology and catalyze our own spiritual evolution.

The first step in such a paradigm shift is gaining an understanding of how life really works. Life, as it turns out, is based not on the guiding hand of a white-robed god floating in the clouds with a stick in his hand, but rather on mathematics, physics, and biology. Life is a fractal. This means it retains its design elements, its core characteristics, at every level of scale. Every living thing, from bacterium and oak tree to elephant, woman, and nation-state, transforms energy. Every living thing reproduces. Every living thing contains DNA. Every living thing moves, every living thing must maintain its harmony and balance, and every living thing evolves.

Long before there were Western academic disciplines, the ancient Chinese philosophy known as Daoism was in possession of these deep truths about life. In the chapters that follow, I will explore how Daoism leverages life's fractal nature, and outline how work at the level of the individual resonates and repeats at the level of the whole world. Specifically, I will detail straightforward personal changes, then changes in attitude, action, and policy, which, when enacted by the billions of individuals planet-wide, could become a single, coherent, magnified force powerful enough to solve famine, drought, abuse, slavery, intolerance, injustice, poverty, violence, environmental devastation, greed, crime, and the scourge of religious fundamentalism.

A nature-based philosophy historically associated with China's intellectual and power elite, yet also popular with artists, merchants, and hermits, Daoism gained coherence during the Axial Age (800 to 200 BC) and reached its apex during China's two most successful and enlightened dynasties, the Han and the Tang. This was the time when China was the world's dominant power and culture, as it is on its way to becoming once again. Unlike ancient traditions that have remained fixed inside static, primitive societies, Daoism grew and deepened over time, gaining sophistication and texture alongside the culture that spawned it. That is because it is fundamentally permeable, having adopted many of the evolving ideas that arose from the long series of invasions, natural disasters, rebellions, and revolutions found in Chinese history.

Among the smorgasbord of the world's great religions, Daoism sits somewhere between the anthropocentric Abrahamic traditions, with their beliefs in a personal god and the importance of sainted interlocutors, and Buddhism, which stresses self-annihilation, the better to free us of ego, attachments, and the suffering they bring. Refined over millennia, Daoism is a philosophy, in relatively recent expansions, a religion, and in its inquiry into nature, a science. Like Western biology, it offers practical directions for living based on how nature works; like sociology it provides guidelines for getting along with others; like psychology, it helps us understand ourselves. Unlike those Western sciences, it combines the various disciplines within a single all-encompassing view.

The word *Dao* means "path" or "way." It is not a road in the physical sense of something we can step onto and follow. Like evolution, or a divine intelligence, it moves things forward and binds them together, but really isn't an "it" at all, being unknowable, omnipresent, and ineffable. It is far too subtle to be a deity to which we can speak or pray, and in this sense is best referred to simply as Dao rather than "the Dao."

In the West today, Daoism is associated with alternative medicine, self-reliance, the Green Movement, a growing awareness of and interest in Chinese culture, and George Lucas' *Star Wars* universe, where spiritually-inclined rebels in search of a just and natural life battle tyrannical, high-tech imperial armies bent upon expansion and conquest. Daoist themes are also increasingly found in rewilding, mindfulness, sustainable agriculture, industry without planned obsolescence, human rights, and self-care. Its circular, black-and-white symbol appears on everything from surf wear to bumper stickers. Interestingly, its Western popularity is even driving a Daoist resurgence in China, revitalizing an important aspect of traditional Chinese culture. International interest in Daoism is also generating the hopeful expectation that this edgy, out-of-the-book form of ancient wisdom might just be able to heal the world.

Daoists don't believe in any separation between man and nature. Abuse of nature, therefore, is tantamount to abusing ourselves. Indeed, because its seeds sprouted in Neolithic proto-China, a time when men and women lived in necessary and intimate association with nature, Daoism may be the original environmentalism. Daoism sees everything in the known and unknown universe as part of an interconnected fabric characterized by a cyclical, balanced, and harmonious interplay between opposing forces or qualities known as *yin* and *yang*. *Yin* is associated with the feminine, dark, heavy, mysterious, and slow; *yang*, with the male, bright, weightless, obvious, and quick. *Yin* and *yang* are not static qualities, but rather are fluid concepts constantly shifting, changing places, dancing, one becoming the other in a myriad of different ways. Many recent discoveries in quantum mechanics, theoretical physics, astronomy, cosmology, and mathematics support this fluid, not-merely-binary model, along with the concept of multiple layers of reality, or multiverses found in very early Daoist thought.

Daoism's growing popularity worldwide likely arises from the way it generates a community of like-minded people who have found its tenets practical and usable as both a spiritual system and recipe for living. Using intellection, meditation, and physical practice, its adherents develop calm, clear minds and an abiding sense of the rationally unfathomable fabric out of which our world is made. This peaceful state serves as a welcome antidote to the frenzy of modern living, and to the disenfranchised sense of alienation and isolation that leads many people to depression and despair. It counters both the personal and societal challenges arising from beliefs that Planet Earth is all about us.

Daoism's shamanic emphasis on understanding natural cycles and energetics also puts it very much in tune with the modern science of biology, particularly when it comes to the nuanced relationship between body and mind. Thousands of years before the field of epigenetics was coined, Daoism addressed the same processes that branch of science studies today— namely, the way our environment can shape our beliefs and moods, and how those mental states can in turn change our physical bodies. Modern scientists engaged in basic research, driven by curiosity rather than corporate or government directive, are doing the same work early Daoists did when they closely observed nature. Perhaps it is this underlying link that allows Daoism to exist as a complement to modern science rather than standing in opposition to it like so many other world religions.

Over time, Daoists cultivate what are known as the Three Treasures: compassion, frugality, and humility. Daoists see these as our natural inclination, the way we saw things, and behaved, during simpler times, before agriculture and industry, when we were able to more easily fit in with the unfolding of nature. It was then, and it is now, perfectly normal to be sensitive to the feelings, wants, and needs of others, utterly regular to be careful with resources, and quite effortless to be humble when we realize our tiny place in the universe and our insignificant role in the unfolding of history. These are not, therefore, qualities to strive for but rather ones that exist within us at all times. No matter how violent, unpredictable, or treacherous the seas of life may prove, Daoism teaches us that if we but lightly seek these qualities under our skins, we will find them in ample supply.

Religious Daoism exists in pockets across China. It features multiple lineages and sects. These answer to no central authority, do not exclude other belief systems (Daoists who are also Buddhists are common), and do not proselytize. This expression of Daoism, however, stands apart from the focus of this book, which is on the philosophical principles that both antedate and underpin its ritual manifestations. Beyond this enormously powerful body of wisdom, Daoism is also interesting for its far-flung community, and for the fact that its adherents enjoy reduced preoccupation with material things and a rekindling of their inner light.

Living a Daoist lifestyle means staying cool, calm, and collected, all the while sensing the unfolding of events and the subtle energies at work in the world. This rock-steady, insightful state is so personally rewarding, it may be the primary driver of the global Daoist awakening. Daoists call this state *wuji*, the same term used to describe a step in the Daoist cosmogony, or creation story. Analogous to the void from which God created heaven and earth as chronicled in the Book of Genesis, *wuji* is a state of perfect stillness—empty but pregnant with infinite possibility. In *wuji*, anything and everything is about to happen, but nothing yet has.

When the Greek conqueror Alexander the Great entered the Phrygian capital of Gordium (in what is now Turkey), he was presented with a knot so thick and tight, nobody could untangle it. His answer was to slice through it with his blade.

Our prejudices, limitations, habits, and beliefs are our own version of that Gordian Knot. We can spend lifetimes trying to untangle it, or we can cut through it in one fell stroke, returning to *wuji* by bringing *yin* and *yang* into balance within ourselves and then in the world outside. The process of returning to *wuji* is called *tai chi*, part of the name for the increasingly popular martial art that serves as the backbone for my personal Daoist practice.

Another way in which I personally cultivate *wuji* is to guide others in doing the work the world requires. That is the purpose of this manifesto. I may not be able to physically restore tropical rainforests, save whales, end factory farming, prosecute the cause of global birth control, wipe out tyranny and the poisonous concept of the free market, educate the ignorant, and help to see wealth redistributed worldwide, but I can certainly have an effect on the intentions of those who are in positions to achieve these goals.

A summary of my apparently unlikely trajectory from Manhattanite to monk shows why it was not really so very unlikely after all. That's because I was born a seeker. While certain folks swim hard and fast against the river of life, others navel-gaze on the bank, and some simply float along without a care, seekers yearn to know what secrets lie beneath the river's surface. We, seekers, are a suspicious lot. We distrust glib and facile answers, and we doubt what we're told about the world. We worry that, if we conform to social norms, we will lose touch with the truths buried deep inside our own consciousness and want to dig for those truths. While many people focus their efforts on career, money, luxury, fame, sex, family, and community, seekers are driven to discover their own true natures, and that of the world.

As a child growing up in the home of a famous physician, I found some of the people around me—scientists, teachers, artists, even a Nobel Peace Prize laureate—to be genuine and compassionate. Yet others, often the richest and most famous, struck me as vainglorious and narcissistic. More to the point, I sensed waves of disquiet in them. They went to prison for tax evasion. They killed their wives. They were depressed. Their children hated them. They committed suicide. Even so, the general population seemed enchanted by their celebrity lives. This made no sense to me, and set me to questioning the prevailing social narrative.

If what I was being told about wealth and fame and power was suspect, might other tales be equally dubious? What about religion and politics? What about life and death? If business is really the primary way in which people interact, should personal profit really be its *sine qua non*? What about equal opportunity for every color and creed? What about social contracts and class warfare? Questioning memes and mores set me to looking at larger issues. Is America's role as beneficent policeman to the world accurate, for example, or are we simply a self-serving empire? What about socialism and communism? Is the military campaign against drugs truly necessary? Are spiritual people just too dumb to be scientists? Is it a good thing that specialization has extinguished the age of the renaissance man or woman?

Having lost so very many family members in Adolf Hitler's Holocaust, it may be that rebelliousness and righteous indignation are lodged in my genetic memory. My grandmother was the sole surviving member of her family of gifted Viennese intellectuals and musicians. My father's luminous career began with a very real struggle to simply survive, his childhood darkened by the looming threat of genocide. Even after the Second World War came to a close, the burbling of anti-Semitism had every Jew fearing a loud knock on the door in the middle of the night. Life seemed so fragile and fraught, the individual so powerless, that assuming a dubious, even cynical posture seemed about right. As a teenager, I became prickly, obstinate, stubborn, and indomitable. I favored my middle finger over all others.

And then I saw my first Bruce Lee movie.

I was immediately entranced. Here, in the brand-new category of kung fu superhero, was empowerment and invulnerability of an exotic and marvelous kind—accessible, too, at least compared to flying around in tights and a cape. Nobody was dragging Bruce to the gas chambers, nor were they abducting David Carradine's character, Kwai Chang Caine, ass-kicking star of the TV show *Kung Fu*. Out of left field or, more precisely, out of a fantasy version of China, came the precise steering wheel I needed to make a sudden left turn in my life. A sickly child, I wasn't strong and healthy enough to actually do Chinese martial arts, but I could certainly become an armchair gladiator.

And I could learn from books. Fascinated by the monks on *Kung Fu*—though never dreaming I would one day become one—I read widely on Buddhism, Confucianism, and Daoism, thereby discovering the glue that has held China together longer than any other continuously-existing culture on the planet. I especially noted the tension between the latter two systems of thought. Confucianism prescribes top-down authority; Daoism stresses the debt a leader owes to his people. Confucianism respects fixed social roles: Daoism emphasizes *wu wei*—relaxed, effortless, unconstrained natural living. Confucianism legislates loyalty and respect for others; Daoism prizes self-expression and the bonds that arise naturally between people.

Famous not only for their ability to see to the heart of nature and the affairs of men, but also for their martial and sexual prowess, the first Daoists were Bacchanalian men and women. Worshippers of nature and connoisseurs of the sensual, they were equally likely to be found legislating at a high level of the imperial court, meditating for a month in a cold mountain cave, or engaging in a bout of orgiastic revelry in the forest. Quietly influential and powerful, they were scholars, librarians, archers, swordsmen, generals, and fortune-tellers to kings. Their emphasis on the human sensorium of sound, sight, touch, taste, and smell led many to become poets and painters in the wilderness school, keen renderers of the beauty of nature and man's tiny role within it. In their view, nature has already addressed the problems with which people so tightly grapple, and has found solutions to all of them. There is no need, according to the Daoist way, to replay that well-sorted drama. Everything we need, from personal guidance to political principles, exists right before us in the natural world. Our only job is to pay attention and follow the cues.

Through all my childhood readings, I most loved the flat-out weirdness of Laozi's *Daodejing*, Daoism's foundational classic: its rebelliousness, irrepressibility, fearless insistence on the existence of higher laws and principles, revolutionary defiance of authoritarian intrusiveness, and perhaps, most of all, its shamanic roots and resultant emphasis on nature, intuition, mysticism, and transcendence. Daoism, it turned out, gave a framework to the revolution I somehow sensed was required in the West. It cut right to the bone of everything.

This is not a memoir, so I have omitted much about my personal journey. Though I remain far less than the man I one day hope to be, I've seen great and terrible things, traveled the world, lost one wife to a car accident, and gained another with whom I've raised a fine son. I've been persecuted in ugly ways and seen family members die horrific deaths. I've watched my parents sadly decline, said goodbye to my father, and endured mortal challenges to my own health. I have been a park ranger, corporate executive, advertising copywriter, management ramrod, zookeeper, screenwriter, speaker, novelist, martial artist, philosophy teacher, and, most importantly, monk. I have spent decades studying Daoist arts with a brilliant master and shared those arts and ideas with an audience of thousands (millions if you include my work on television).

Despite the dark and dire start to this introduction, I do not believe it is necessary to let the obfuscating razzle-dazzle of what we call civilization, with its lap dogs—culture, society, and politics—stop us from listening to our intuition about what is right and true and kind and important. I believe that, by acknowledging our miniscule role in an infinite landscape, as Daoist artists do, we can step off the path of widespread pain, suffering, and injustice and onto one of joy, equality, compassion, and mutual respect. Philosophically and spiritually, we are evolving in the direction of being able to do this. Evolution is not a linear process. Rather, it radiates in all directions, producing a wide range of beautiful examples of intelligence, physical capacities, shapes, sizes, and strategies.

Among other important improvements, we are increasingly sensitive to what we are doing to the planet. More, though still abused around the world, human rights have at least become a subject of major discussion and concern. We have abolished slavery in most places. Women are slowly but increasingly left in charge of their own bodies. Domestic violence, racism, and sexism are coming into the critical spotlight of public opinion. We are starting to recognize that substance abuse is a disease and that mental illness is not a character deficit. We are questioning the torture and consumption of sentient beings. We are facing corruption's corrosive presence in our governments and societies. Perhaps, most significantly, we are finally, though again too slowly, recognizing the poison in religious extremism and other fictions of faith.

We have reached the point in our evolution where our survival depends upon us coming to understand how our minds work, how our minds drive our behavior, and how our behavior affects the world. Every ill in the world begins as an illness inside a human being, and every human illness has an emotional and spiritual element. Mahatma Gandhi, not a Daoist but a person who understood, as most spiritual people do, the link between our minds and our world, declared: "Be the change that you wish to see in the world." More profound and beautiful words have rarely been spoken. To counter the catastrophes of our time, we must address our chaotic compendium of personal confusions. We must peel back layer after layer of misunderstanding, self-indulgence, lack of discipline, misguided beliefs, and pathological disconnection from the natural world. The fruit of such internal resolution is external revolution. In a world of awakened human beings, so much of what is flat-out wrong can no longer stand. If we can evolve fast enough, we can tip the scales back in favor of our species, and of the rest of the world, too.

The blueprint that follows is based on the notion of building a strong body as a foundation for an awakened mind, then using that mind to assume personal responsibility and fully awaken the self. This prescription applies even when fortune fades, moods change, circumstances worsen, and titillation dims. It emphasizes connecting with others (once we have done the work to repair damage to ourselves) and then with all of nature. It includes both hints for personal spiritual hygiene and sweeping political creeds melded together in what is the quintessence of Daoism. All this may seem mad in the sense of crazy, utopian, naïve, outrageous, extreme, unrealistic, quixotic, and hopelessly romantic, but Daoists have followed this path for millennia and never found it lacking.

I believe that the most effective way to help each other onto the path is to foster constructive dialog, particularly with those in other "tribes," about what matters most to them and their communities. The increasing number of seemingly impenetrable borders between us—including religious fundamentalism, greed and self-interest on a national scale, and, not least, tech-centered communication that minimizes altruism and empathy—have deprived us of such dialogs, substituting for them superficial exchanges that are quite often more bombast and bluster than compassionate substance. If we could use the ideas in this manifesto as a starting point for sustained, open, and positive channels of communication, we would certainly do better than could any top-down cohering force (an oxymoron if there ever was one), much better than any biblical or alien savior, and much better than any future digital overlord.

Ancient masters of Way
all subtle mystery and dark-enigma vision:
they were deep beyond knowing,

so deep beyond knowing
we can only describe their appearance:

Perfectly cautious, as if crossing winter streams,
and perfectly watchful, as if neighbors threatened;
perfectly reserved, as if guests,
perfectly expansive, as if ice melting away,
and perfectly simple as if uncarved wood;
perfectly empty, as if open valleys,
and perfectly shadowy, as if murky water.

Who's murk enough to settle slowly into pure clarity,
and who still enough to awaken slowly into life?

If you nurture this Way, you never crave fullness.
never crave fullness
and you'll wear away into completion.

—Laozi Stanza 15[1]

---

1   David Hinton, *Tao Te Ching*, Berkeley, California: Counterpoint, 2015.

NOTES ON
THE PRESENTATION

I have woven together what I hope you will find a compelling and informative handbook for achieving personal evolution that leads to peaceful social revolution. I would like to think that the process of reading, considering, and sharing the ideas herein can catalyze true change in you and organically generate those vaunted qualities of humility, frugality, and compassion. The flow of things is as follows:

- Specific personal and political calls to action

- Inspirational references

- Key snippets from Chinese history

- A philosophical travel guide

- Stories about the transformational power of Daoist ideas

- Teachings of famous sages

In presenting the material, I follow the exact model Daoist practice does, namely the precise progression from considering the work we do on ourselves to considering how that work affects the world. Accordingly, we begin with relaxing and rectifying the physical body, move to awakening our minds, proceed to contributing to community and improving culture, continue to consider how Daoist ideas manifest in culture, commerce, and government, review the relationship between sensitivity and the environment, and finally engage with the role of spirit and service in an awakened life. Within each section, there are thematically arranged groups, with the occasional stubborn thought that may not fit perfectly with the others but deserves consideration nonetheless.

As you read, please remember that truth is invariably more complicated than we like it to be, that there are layers upon interrelated layers to what we call reality. Things are often smaller, larger, constantly shifting, a piece of something else, and an intersection of happenings and forces. There is always a great unfolding. I hope you'll think deeply about these ideas, share them with others, and season them with the wisdom of your own insights and experience.

There are a variety of systems to transliterate Chinese to English. The Chinese government's standard *Pinyin* system, despite some awkwardness, is rapidly becoming the gold standard, so I have cleaved to it in this book. Each section ends with a quote from the much-vaunted *Daodejing*. I have chosen my favorite translations of the many available in English, so as to render the old master as widely and clearly as possible through various voices.

In anticipation of your kind attention, I offer nine grateful bows.

CHAPTER ONE

RELAXING
AND RECTIFYING

The seventeenth-century French philosopher René Descartes launched centuries of confusion about neuroanatomy and the reality of material existence with the famous dictum: "I think, therefore I am." Daoist experience instantiates a contravening notion, namely that all distinctions between body and mind are specious. Some years ago, I attended a traveling exhibit called "BODIES: The Exhibition," which revealed human structures in their full glory through the injection of liquid plastics that filled up and fleshed out all our systems. Perhaps the most startling revelation of the exhibit was the fact that the nervous system is not merely the brain and spinal cord, but rather, a vast, jellyfish-like array of tissue that pervades us from top to bottom, innervating our organs, including our digestive tract—where a second brain, the size of a cat, gives us our so-called "gut feelings"—as well as the skin on the very tips of our fingers and toes.

Beyond anatomy, proof that the brain and body are inextricably interdigitated comes from both anecdotes and experiments that demonstrate the mortal effects of either fearing or wishing for impending death. Most recently, experiments in the field of epigenetics—beginning by stressing colonies of bacteria and progressing to examining changes in human DNA pursuant to various forms of stress—illustrate definitively that our emotions play a key part in gene expression, turning up and down the "volume" on the expression of genetic characteristics, ranging from a predisposition to cancer to the course of puberty and other developmental changes. Given the inseparability of the body and mind, the Daoist axiom that heightened consciousness and increased awareness depend upon a strong body makes perfect sense.

The body may or may not be the temple of the soul, but we completely rely upon it either way. In the Daoist ideal, a healthy body is relaxed, soft, pliable, and yielding. Like a palm tree bending in a storm, our softness allows us to endure life's harsh winds and strong storms. There are passages in Laozi's *Daodejing* that exhort us not only to recover the simple innocence of childhood but also to find in adult life the physical suppleness we had as infants, when our limbs could be led, naturally and without training, into postures to rival any yogini's. In contrast to a palm tree, an oak can grow a fine and showy canopy but, by virtue of being rigid, will snap when assailed by weather or even by climbing children.

Once the body is relaxed, we can begin to rectify it. Rectification of the body means setting things straight by implementing new and positive changes. We fix our posture, straighten our spine, and treat physical inflammation or dysfunction primarily with diet and exercise. We integrate the body from hand to foot, meaning that any work done with our hands while standing is subtly felt in every part of the body, all the way to the feet. We gain that sensitivity through relaxation, meditation, and the cultivation of simple habits, like moving back as far as possible in our chair while sitting, so as to work the abdominal muscles that give us the strength to maintain this position.

Our next step is to rectify the mind. This means inspecting our habits, our preconceptions, tendencies, foibles, beliefs, and whatever limitations we unnecessarily accept. By carefully considering so much of what we all take for granted, we move off the stultifying platform of certainty and comfort and into the realm of healthy questioning and unease. This is a healthy place, despite the challenges, and good prescriptions naturally arise from dwelling in it.

The magnificent Daoist sage, Zhuangzi, is generally believed to have lived during the fourth century BC. His short stories, together comprising one of the earliest works of Asian literature, are well known to every Chinese schoolchild. In one of the most famous passages of Eastern philosophy, he meets a friend at an inn for tea and recounts a dream in which he was a butterfly zooming across the landscape, flapping his beautiful wings and enjoying the power, freedom, and perspective of flight. He tells his friend he isn't entirely sure whether he is a man who has just dreamed he was a butterfly, or a butterfly who is now dreaming he is a man.

This preoccupation with identity—the nature of individual existence and the rectification of the self—is a hallmark of Daoism. Indeed, the great preponderance of Daoist practice is focused on the self—not in a narcissistic way, but rather in pursuit of consciousness, service, and immortal Dao running through all that is. This practice is done primarily through physical and meditative exercises, which expand the mind, sharpen the senses, and increase longevity. There are also rituals, including chants, arcane sexual practices, and reading of the classics, all of which encourage the light of truth to enter even the darkest corners of the mind.

I knew quite a few exercises but not so many rituals, at least until the day I became a monk. On that day, South China steamed. The temple, once a rural property but now lodged squarely in the middle of the huge city's garment district, was such a walled-in hotbox that even the trees begged for a breeze. The day-long ordination ritual began in the relative cool of morning but, as the day progressed, the wooden beams in the high-ceiling temple chambers in which we chanted, bowed, prayed, and rang bells began to sweat.

Unlike many ancient systems of thought, which have remained fixed inside static, "primitive" societies, Daoism has grown and deepened over time, gaining sophistication and texture alongside the culture that spawned it. This means adopting and integrating ideas from other traditions as needed. In the glaring eyes of hundreds of deities set in alcoves around me, I saw evidence of Confucian ancestor worship and Buddhist beliefs in statues brightly painted in yellow, gold, blue, green, black, and red, and rendered in half-man-size, seemingly swollen with tears. In their midst were more than a few renderings of the Buddha himself and of his female counterpart Guanyin, Goddess of Mercy.

Some water was available, but not more than a sip here or there. My fellow monks seemed less uncomfortable than I was, perhaps because they had long ago acclimated to wearing robes in the tropical heat. As the devotional ritual unfolded, they watched me, took care of me, led me from chamber to chamber and building to building. My command of Chinese was not nearly good enough to quickly and precisely read the characters before me, so I mostly mumbled and stumbled through hours of chants read from texts rendered in ancient, thick-paged books.

The texts before me were specific to the somewhat newer branch of Daoism in which I was being ordained, which differed from the older branch I'd been raised on through Master Yan's martial arts. My first and strongest loyalty was to Master Yan but I knew I was lucky to have Master Pan, and through him, a second lineage in which to study and to grow. Historically associated with poets, artists, merchants, and hermits, Daoism is also popular with China's intellectual and power elite, and I'd seen such people floating in and out of Pan's private office.

Serene, sedate, rotund, and blessed with a breeze from the flat bamboo fans of acolytes attending him, long thick black hair tucked under his square, Daoist hat, Pan looked on. I worried I was disappointing him, but I needn't have. When it was time to receive my certificate at the end of the day, I found myself bowing prostrated before him,

*hands and knees on a maroon pillow, thumbs hidden so as to evoke
the yin/yang symbol known as the* taijitu. *When the signal came,
I stood and bowed three times, paused, did the same again, paused,
and did one last set of three, for a total of nine gestures of obeisance.
Halfway through, despite downcast eyes, I caught a glimpse of Pan's
expression—an admixture of curiosity and affection, conveying
without words the question, "Crazy foreigner, what are you
doing here?"*

*The last time, however, he gave me a smile I can only describe as
beatific. I felt his positive energy, his encouragement and affection,
as clearly as a laser beam from his eyes. Daoist masters have for
millennia provided a wellspring of wisdom based on close study of
nature and, in that capacity, have served as influential advisors to
China's rulers. I thought about the long road I'd taken, from a New
York City apartment to this incense-filled Chinese temple. I bathed in
the light of Pan's approbation and felt a rise of satisfaction at having
followed my path of self-cultivation to this memorable and marvelous
time and place.*

TUNING IN THE WORLD

To really understand the flavor of classical Daoist wisdom, it's
best to open the mind by reading regularly from the Daoist
canon. Some of the major works therein have been translated
from their original Chinese. These include the divinatory,
philosophical catalog of natural unfoldings, the *Yijing*, the
famous *Daodejing* (The Classic of the Way and Virtue), the
Zhuangzi (The Classic of Master Zhuang), *Huangting Jing* (The
Classic of the Yellow Court), *Taiyi Jinhua Zongzhi* (The Secret
of the Golden Flower), the *Qing Jingjing* (The Classic of Purity
and Stillness), and the *Huainanzi* (Master Huainan, a wise,

encyclopedic collection of instructions for ruling a country that employs the very same root-and-branches structure as this manifesto). Daoist adherents find the principles and ideas in these books so compelling they adopt Daoist choices, priorities, diet, and values. Using intellection, meditation, and physical practice, they develop calm, clear minds and an abiding sense of the rationally unfathomable fabric of which our world is made. Why not take a stab at one and see what insights it reveals?

· · ·

Airline safety announcements counsel us to put on our own oxygen mask before assisting others. The Daoist version of putting on the mask is the process of growing healthy, calm, and clear, balancing our urges so as to grow wise, realize our potential, and become a sage. A sage is a person who deeply senses the flow of the world and moves with it, not against it. Sages recognize the inherent wisdom of nature, the long-term genius of universal forces. We have gone beyond book-learning to a different kind of knowing. Quintessentially wise, we seem to do nothing, yet somehow get everything done. At any given moment, we may appear fools, maybe even idiots, and yet, in the fullness of time, we are revealed to be anything but. We are soft, yielding, and relaxed, yet often triumph; we covet nothing, yet have all we need; we seek to control no one but ourselves, yet are sought out for counsel; we consider ourselves nothing special, yet are in primary and constant contact with ineffable Dao.

· · ·

Exercising the brain is as important as exercising the body. Despite the digital training currently in vogue, the best kind of mental exercise takes place neither in front of screen nor in front of printed page, but with eyes closed, ears guarded, safety assured, and with clean, fresh air without wind. This exercise is called meditation, and there is an increasing body of literature pertaining to its myriad of health benefits. One of these is that meditation improves the *physical* condition of the brain, just as exercise tones and strengthens the body. While meditation can be used as a tool to accomplish a number of different goals, Daoists use it to bring mind and body into harmonious union. Sitting or lying-down meditation will do, but standing meditation most strongly encourages the flow of energy up the back and down the front of the body in what we call the Great Heavenly Circle. Folding our hands over our navel (left hand on top for men, right hand on top for women), we position our feet shoulder-width apart. Relaxing the torso, we settle into the support of our pelvic girdle, our knees slightly soft, eyes gently closed, tip of our tongue comfortably resting just above and behind the front teeth. Suspended between Earth and sky in the classic natural position for the human animal, we breathe through our nose and concentrate on progressively relaxing our body from top to bottom, in horizontal cross sections, like the rings on a stalk of bamboo. Let's try it today for a minute, tomorrow for two, and then the next day for three. Let's keep adding a minute per day until, at the end of the month, the session lasts half an hour. Substitute this exercise for a meal three times per week. The benefits include a calmer, less reactive mind and a stronger, healthier body—all qualities of the rectified body/mind.

. . .

Many of the ills of the world arise from our fundamental inability to simply stand quietly and wait for the next unfolding. Before committing to any consequential action, let's wait, be patient, take a breath, and reconsider.

. . .

If there is a single beneficial thing we can do for our body and our mind that utterly transcends any system of beliefs, any spiritual, religious, cultural, or social context, it is to learn to breathe. Breathing is the first thing we do upon entering this existence, and the last as well. The fact that most of us don't know how to do it, that we breathe about as well as a one-legged man in flip flops runs a marathon, is, indeed, a sad sign of the effects of modern living. We know how to breathe when we are born, of course. As babies, we breathe with our bellies. In goes the air as the belly expands, pulling the diaphragm downward and creating negative pressure in the lungs. Out goes the air as the belly contracts, the diaphragm lifts, and the air is squeezed out of the lungs. As the stresses of our speed-and-greed world begin to intrude, sometimes as early as kindergarten, we forget about the belly and resort to using the chest muscles, a short term, emergency tactic our ancestors used to flee from saber-tooth cats and like predators. All this breathing with the wrong muscles prolongs our stress response and exhausts us. Let's start paying attention to our breathing today. Let's notice if we are using our belly or our chest, and if it's our chest, let's move all the action down lower, where it belongs. This is the first step in learning to relax.

. . .

Because we are complex biological and spiritual beings, we are subject to the effects of countless, constantly shifting inner and outer forces. Sensing the world around us with trained eyes, ears, touch, and tongue, we can everywhere see *yin* and *yang* in an intimate dance. The binary on-off position of switches is what makes our digital world possible, for example, and the gradual swap of winter and summer defines our yearly cycle. While we might be tempted to focus on the simple duality of this setup—the existence of opposites in all things and the tension between them—it is actually the way the two opposites change positions, like kings on a chess board defecting to the other player's side, that defines this universal game. There is no *yang* without *yin*, no *yin* without *yang*, and one is constantly in the process of becoming the other. Thus, in noticing what causes us stress and what helps us relax, who supports us in our work to grow and improve and who holds us back, we can create our own balance and move ourselves forward. There is *yin* and *yang* to relaxation, see, and to rectification as well. Embracing this truth, we can create harmonious lives filled with compassion, wisdom, and awareness of resources.

. . .

The more "real" technology makes the virtual world feel, the more it diverges from the Daoist experience. Videogame headsets shaking with the bass notes of gunshots and bombs disconnect us from each other at a time when connection is precisely what we need to heal the rifts between us and save the world. Love is the antidote to environmental Armageddon, yet we daily withdraw from nature and spend more time attached to artificial worlds. Let's rekindle our relationship with nature instead of upping our game score. Let's joyfully experience the natural world, the oceans, the jungles, the forests, the deserts, the salt water, the steaming vines, the tall trees, the cactus spines, the glorious sunsets, and the sand between our toes. How about we log out of the game and get back in touch with our one, true home?

. . .

Before the dawn of agriculture, people didn't see that much of each other, at least by today's standards. They hunted, gathered in groups for a time, then dispersed and went their merry way. Today, people are crammed together. The result is that the tangible, biological need for solitude and quiet goes unanswered. Time spent alone in the wilderness is essential to human health and an integral part of the Daoist rectification process and lifestyle. This does not necessarily mean rigorous hiking or camping trips, nor does it require expensive travel to exotic destinations. A simple walk in the woods will do, and if no woods are available, then time spent in a park. Finding parks crowded, we may wish to venture out early in the morning or late in the evening, so long as it is safe to do so. Such restorative forays are a wonderful addition to our routine during any season of the year, and often provide the distance from our problems needed to generate fresh ideas and solutions.

. . .

Sound is a form of energy and can affect the molecular bonds that cohere solid matter. In extreme cases, like when an opera singer shatters a champagne glass by singing a high C, sound may be disruptive. Yet sound can also be beneficial, as when ultrasound is used to penetrate tissue and treat chronic pain. Many religions utilize chanting to generate a meditative state of mind, and the idea of music as therapy is accepted widely enough to have generated a medical discipline. Kung Fu styles, notably the one originating at the famed Shaolin Temple, even incorporates loud and deliberate vocalizations into martial arts practice.

In addition to techniques such as acupuncture, herbs, meditation, and qigong, Daoist medicine uses vibrations created with our vocal cords to benefit our organs and organ systems. Such functional and energetic benefits are propounded by Daoism's Five Element Healing System, which describes the way our body works in metaphorical terms, with wood, metal, earth, fire, and water as the currency of change.

The Six Healing Sounds comprise a simple and manageable set of prescriptive techniques to benefit the liver, heart, kidneys, lungs, spleen, and digestion. It is worth noting that, from the Chinese medical point of view, the spleen is a function rather than an organ, and the benefits of sound-making to digestion center around an organ system known as the "Triple Burner," which has no direct analog in Western anatomy.

As is true with many Daoist healing techniques, the Six Healing Sounds take into account not only the cycles of growth, aging, and healing in the body, but also the larger natural cycles of the seasons. The sounds are quite fun to do and will produce results if practiced over a period of weeks and months. To start, practice making the sound aloud, to refine clarity and accuracy. Once mastered, try making it more quietly, letting the breath do as much of the work as the vocal cords. This means that the second set of six should be done more as a whisper than a shout. I have found it best to practice each sound six times, adding an additional six repetitions when the organ system is "in season," or to address a particular health problem in the relevant area. The sounds are:

1. *Liver. Spring Season. Wood. **"Shhhhh."** Wood grows in spring and the liver is more active during that season. If the liver is weak, illnesses such as hepatitis may arise at that time.*

2. *Heart. Summer. Fire. "**Kuhhhh.**" Fire happens in summer and the heart is active during that period. Same medical logic as above.*

3. *Spleen. Transition between seasons. Earth. "Hoooo." Same medical logic as above.*

4. *Lung. Autumn. Metal. "**Sssszz.**" This sound has a buzz at the end. Same medical logic as above.*

5. *Kidney system. Winter. Water. "**Chuaay.**" Same medical logic as above.*

6. *Triple Burner/Heater/Warmer (digestion). All seasons. "**Ssss.**" All elements.*

. . .

Noise pollution is an oft-overlooked culprit in the chronic, lifestyle-based diseases of modern society. Even those who are accustomed to noise, and temporarily uncomfortable with quiet, eventually experience lower heart and respiratory rates in a tranquil environment. Rectification requires some silence, for in silence, we confront our true nature and the sources of our stress, finding within ourselves creativity and spirituality, too. There are all kinds of things we can do to make our lives quieter, including the use of earplugs while flying, sleeping, and working, closing windows to reduce street noise, and reducing the volume on our speakers and headphones. We might also lobby to outlaw blowing car horns in urban areas, and levy fines on drivers who modify mufflers or don't repair damaged ones, introduce nighttime fly-over legislation for communities near airports, enforce construction bans at night and on weekends, and encourage replacing leaf blowers with rakes. While we're at it, let's diminish background music in public spaces like malls and elevators, and reintroduce soft, courteous speech, too. Let's go back to considering loud people boorish instead of encouraging them by paying them extra attention.

• • •

A great deal is made these days about the electrical nature of our bodies. This may be a direct consequence of our obsession with digital doodads and the unfolding of virtual worlds we have created in order to escape from the dire mess we've made of this real one. In addition to electricity, however, there is another form of energy with which we can express ourselves, and which is an integral part of who we are. That energy is light, and its units are photons, not electrons. Photons saturate our world, originate in the sun and distant stars (long burned out, by the way, but still sending us their celestial glory), and enter our bodies through both our eyeballs and our skin. The great fabric of existence is bolstered by the ongoing exchange of these photons—the fact that every time we look at each other, every time we so much as share visible space, we share photons instantly and pervasively. We give them to each other. They are gifts that knit together space and time. What we feel, intend, and do are all part of, and are actively contributing to, a vast landscape of light. Seen this way, photons can even be considered building blocks in the creation of a new self.

• • •

When considering relaxation and rectification both, let's remember that we are not a single coherent entity, but instead a lively festival of worms, protozoa, molds, amoeba, bacteria, virus, and fungi—all cooperating over the course of our lifespan so as to simply survive. In fact, only 43 percent of the cells in our bodies are human! Each of the billions of organisms living within us has a role to play, and many are absolutely essential to the life of the host. Recent research into the wide-ranging importance of the flora and fauna in our gut is an example of how we are reordering our understanding of what it means to be human and what it means to be alive. More research into the genetic variability of this microbiome will likely lead to breakthrough treatments for a wide range of diseases. In the meantime, why not turn our meditative attention to the divine cacophony of tiny agendas, all being exercised upon our will and our well-being, so as to better understand who and what we really are? We can do this by experimenting with our microbiome through the use of food and supplements, but in seeking profound growth and change, it wouldn't hurt to mentally ask for permission and assistance from all the little beings who make us who we are.

THE WAY WE FEEL

We must often yield so as to gain greater understanding and ultimately triumph; sometimes, on the way to both relaxation and rectification, it's to our advantage to sometimes invest in loss, meaning give up some ground to gain some later or accept the loss of a battle the better to win the war. We must be willing to let go of people and things and ideas. We must never directly fight force with force, but rather spiral around obstacles. To see spiral movement in action, one has only to look through a good telescope and see what happened when the detritus from exploding stars and the rushing material of creation crashed together eons ago, leaving us spiral galaxies. It also happens that spiraling is the most effective way to move liquid through a solid matrix, which is why authentic tai chi is remarkably effective in aiding the circulation of blood and lymph through our body's matrix of soft tissue and bone. The spiral, in short, is nature's way of managing conflict.

. . .

Letting go is simultaneously the easiest and most difficult thing in the world to do. Easy, because it is simple, effortless, and natural; difficult because grasping is inherent in our lifestyle. We are commanded by corrosive religious traditions that tell us we are imperfect and must constantly strive to be godly or even worthy. This manipulative and twisted lie causes us to prize obstinacy and obedience over sensitivity, and to collide with difficult people and situations rather than circumnavigate them. If we are to evolve to the next stage of consciousness, we must relax, quit struggling, and accept ourselves as microcosmically flawed but macrocosmically perfect.

. . .

It is often hard to relax when we feel assaulted by daily stresses and pressures. These forces arise from a limited and often negative life narrative, one we have learned the way we learned language and customs and culture. The narrative is at best the partial truth about ourselves and our lives. Our planet is only a tiny speck in the cosmos and yet, even here, we miss so very much because of the limitations of our eyes, ears, noses, fingertips, and tongues. Lacking sonar, for example, we cannot detect bugs on the fly in a dark cave the way a bat can. We cannot feel the water column above us the way a deep-sea lamprey does, nor sense the electrical discharges of prey after the fashion of sharks, skates, and rays. We will never hear songs sent our way through thousands of miles of water by our cetacean kin. We will never hear the ultra-low-frequency vibrations of other elephants in our herd. Despite the revelations brought to scientists by computers, sensors, telescopes, and microscopes, on a daily basis most of us remain oblivious to the larger workings of the cosmos. Accepting how little we perceive of our world and how little we can therefore understand of it, we can abide in a place of wonder and respect for the world rather than attempting to dominate it.

. . .

We don't all look like supermodels, think like geniuses, earn like moguls, own like sheiks, and rule like kings. Thinking that we do, indeed, thinking that we *should*, distances us from the bitter struggle that is life for billions of people around the globe. So distant, we become lost to greed and self-importance. We become graspers, forever discontented with what we do and what we have. This creates stress, which precludes relaxation. Let's get real: Each of us does indeed have our place and our role in the world, but beyond rights and freedoms and the meeting of our biological needs, we don't deserve a thing! The idea that we deserve anything at all is obnoxious, New Age, politically-correct puffery, and comes at a high price to those around us. It is high time we abandoned self-congratulatory narcissism. Instead, let's frankly appraise our achievements and contributions in the context of a world flattened by globalization and imperiled by thoughtless human domination. When regarding ourselves, let's focus on compassion and community instead of on gratification, self-aggrandizement, and excess. In this way, we rectify ourselves, and restore harmony and balance to a world badly in need of both.

. . .

Energetic exchange is the overarching principle of all human interaction, and there is far more energy in feelings than there is in facts. The sooner we accept emotions to be more powerful (not better or more important) than facts, the sooner we will achieve beneficent government, realistic and effective politics, and a frank understanding of what makes us tick. This represents a move away from the doomed, rational way we try and define ourselves, towards the hot, wet, feeling creatures we actually are, passions and insecurities and ambitions and all. The trick is to judge ourselves less, because we are not the machines some would portray us to be, but rather to accept that we are creatures born of an organic planet and living in an unpredictable and often dangerous world. Rectification is organic; it is not the stuff of stiff, sci-fi cyborgs. When we embrace our own emotional irrationality during the setting of policy and the charting of courses, we actually cleave most closely to nature, finding balance, and relieving our changeable selves of the burdens of unrealistic, rigid, and unchanging strictures and rules.

...

If our culture has one defining characteristic, that characteristic is anger. Americans have the dubious distinction of being amongst the angriest people on earth. Anger doesn't just lead us to kill each other, it also kills each and every one of us. We see the evidence every day. High blood pressure, blown arteries, refluxing digestive systems, insomnia, and more. How can the wealthiest and most privileged society in human history be so angry? The first answer is the sense of entitlement we get from media messages about material abundance and excess: the gap between our lives and the lives we see on television, in movies, and on billboards. The second is the unequal distribution of wealth, healthcare, and education, and the opportunity gaps across racial and socioeconomic divides. The third answer is an all-pervasive lack of awareness of our own good fortune. A dose of reality can lead to gratitude, and gratitude is the best antidote to our individual and collective rage. Grateful, we can begin to relax. Relaxed, we can begin to rectify. Rectifying, we can channel anger into energy for positive action.

. . .

It is long past time to erase the stigma of mental illness. Advances in science and medicine have demonstrated that depression, schizophrenia, and substance abuse are diseases every bit as organic as Alzheimer's or Parkinson's. We should no more discriminate against someone with a broken mind than we would against someone with a broken leg. The cure to mental illness starts with compassion and forbearance on the part of the patient's family, then proceeds to placing the highest priority on their care. Compassion is a key element of the awakened, rectified life.

. . .

While there is a definite role for certain traditional hallucinogens—particularly those from the shamanic tradition—in advancing the growth of consciousness, the dark side of hallucinogens is a bad trip, enduring psychosis, or worse. While Daoists have traditionally availed themselves of nature's toolkit for the maintenance of health and the expansion of consciousness, these days the most popular Daoist methods for achieving these goals are meditation and qigong under the guidance of a qualified master. Too, psychotropic drugs are so widely abused these days and, when abused, can so ravage families and communities, that their use must be weighed carefully against their risks. Addiction is a personal and public health issue. As part of a compassionate society, addiction-avoidance education, ongoing support, and therapy for addicts is the responsibility of government. It must be provided without cost, and funded by corporate profits, consumer taxes, and social programs.

. . .

Feeling entirely certain of our own motivations is a strong sign we are deluding ourselves. Pretty much nothing we do is based on a single, pure emotion or concern. Our feelings are never one-dimensional, our reasons for what we do never simple. Yet understanding our motivation is a big piece of understanding ourselves and an absolute prerequisite to real rectification. As always, step one is to relax. During meditation we have an opportunity to really ask ourselves why we're doing something. In the peace and quiet of the meditative stance, we can find the space to discover the layers of truth in our lives. Experience, perspective, mood, and circumstance lend different shades, casts, and insights to what we see and how we see it. Let's recognize that even feelings or convictions we consider fixed and inviolable may well change or become irrelevant one day. This is because we are subject to cycles, contracting and expanding, rising and falling. The more extreme the highs we reach, the more compensatory the lows will be. The farther to the right we move, the more we can expect a shift to the left, and vice versa. Let's come to see ourselves not as steel but as water, shifting, changing, evolving, reversing and being flexible enough to bend and fold with the times. Daoist rectification is all about being like water.

. . .

Passionate enthusiasm is the greatest source of energy but can also be the antithesis of relaxation. Ramped up, we may think superficial thoughts and make irrational decisions. Instead of becoming lost in feelings of optimism and personal power, why not use the energy passion provides to explore the *yin* and *yang* of our emotional register, the inevitable falling away of a positive mood in favor of a dour one? Can we find reassurance in that cycle? Can we find the passionate times all the more precious because they are fleeting? Can we remember them when we feel down and know they will return? When we feel low, can we relish the opportunity to rectify ourselves in the solemn focus of the moment? When it is time to rest and recuperate, let's do that. When it's time to go crazy, let's do that, too. High or low, let's sense the sublime all-pervasive breathing of the universe—in and out, standing for happy and for sad. This sensing is a passion itself, a passion for Dao.

. . .

The more predictably we behave on the outside, the less likely we are to be in tune with nature. This is because—large forces like magnetism, gravity, and the cycling of seasons aside—the progression of natural events is generally chaotic. Therefore, let's not worry if our desks are messy. Let's not fret if all our tools are not lined up inside drawers. Let's not waste time ordering all the books on our shelves or the songs on our playlists. Let's not take the same route to work every day. Let's not always insist upon the same table at our favorite eatery. Let's not fixate on one brand of shoe to the exclusion of others. Let's not squander our energy attempting to order a fundamentally disordered universe. Instead, let's use meditation and exercise to rectify ourselves, to find what is constant and true within, and thereby create internal coherence and stability. In this way, we will be able to effortlessly flow with the vicissitudes and challenges of life while growing inside in harmony with the ever-expanding universe.

. . .

In groundbreaking research in the latter part of the twentieth century, Nobel laureate Dr. Wilder Penfield attempted to map the connections between specific parts of the body and particular areas of the brain. He wanted to see, for example, where the "wires" from the hand led, and where the connections to the feet ended up. To produce his map, Penfield had to be able to talk to his subjects while working on them. A needle stuck in a particular part of the brain might make a patient feel hungry or make her feel as if her fingers were on fire, but Penfield could only know this if the patient was awake and communicative. Fortunately, while the skull has sensory nerves in it, the brain does not, so Penfield could numb the skull, and go ahead and poke away without causing the patient pain.

Penfield's poking and talking routine gave him the information he was after along with an additional surprise, namely that the patient was able to announce what he was experiencing. Rather than simply saying, "Yum, mustard," for example, the patient was able to say, "When you use that needle, I taste mustard on my tongue." Penfield got to wondering who was speaking and who was the "I" to which the speaker was referring. Put another way, what person was it who was watching the experiment from afar and reporting on the effects of his needle? He realized that in order to phrase things that way, the patient had to be watching the experiment unfold from some place deep either within or high above.

There's more. When Penfield stimulated a place in the brain that made the patient clench his fist, then said, "Look, I'm going to do that again, this time try to resist the clenching," the fist clenched to a lesser extent. Because of the way the patient reacted, Penfield inferred that the person whose hand was moving, and the person who was trying to stop the hand from moving, were in some fashion not one and the same. Penfield called the person he was talking to the "watcher."

Depending upon how much experience we have meditating, we soon discover that we can watch ourselves watch ourselves watch ourselves, and so on. Daoists make the same observation Penfield did and take it a step or two further. In our tradition, the first level of occurrence is the external, objective fact—there is a table. The second level is the sensory register of that fact or event—seeing the table, for instance. The third level is interpreting what we see—"Ah. That's a table." The fourth level is the emotion that arises—"What a beautiful table!" The last, fifth level, applies to our response to the previous four—"I move that table so the puppy doesn't chew on its legs."

Once we understand that there is a watcher, many previously impossible tasks become trivial. Moreover, experiences we may have had, like time slowing down during a mortal encounter of a car accident or shoot-out, make a new kind of sense. Given this hygiene of distance, keeping our equilibrium becomes much, much easier. Dangerous and stressful events have less immediacy, leaving us free to respond rather than react, and to stay calm and make better decisions. Last but not least, we can, at any moment, find new coaches in our efforts to relax and rectify ourselves. We have only to check in with our watchers.

CYCLES AND MOTION

Many Western exercise programs emphasize the way the body looks as opposed to the way it functions, isolating muscle groups with specific exercises and sometimes even puffing us up with artificial nutrients and stimulant drugs. This method appeals more to vanity than to good sense, benefiting appearance over function. Instead, let's see the body and the way it works in terms of systems, not individual organs or anatomical structures. Tai chi, qigong, and the herbs and acupuncture pull together organs, muscles, ligaments, tendons, and bones. Linked properly to the mind, the entire body becomes healthier and stronger, and performance improves. This is *real* rectification.

...

The burgeoning field of epigenetics tells us that our DNA is not a life sentence written in stone, but more a loose guide to our characteristics, health, and disease. As we interact with our environment, our lifestyle, feelings, and thoughts switch our genes on and off. In this heady respect, we literally are what we think and feel. Interactive genetic mutability has health, longevity, and spiritual enlightenment resting upon a foundation of a calm mind and a life lived in *harmony* with nature rather than one in opposition to it. Unquestioningly accepting stereotypes limits us in so very many ways. The narratives we tell ourselves about our physical abilities, the inevitability of our genetics, the limitations of our circumstances and educations, are all wrong and needlessly constrain us. Relaxing turns off dangerous genes. Rectifying ourselves means understanding that while our genetic code may be written, how it is expressed depends upon our reactions to stress and what we do to reject what others have told us are our limits. The first step in growing past old boundaries, breaking old bonds, and rejecting stories we tell ourselves and stereotypes others apply to us is to understand that we are changing and evolving in each moment of our lives. The step after that is to take conscious and deliberate control of that change through the various suggestions offered here.

. . .

The inevitability of aging turns out to be a fallacy. Despite popular belief, older people's brains don't become slow and weak but rather more densely packed with information. Experience does this to us. It creates new webs of association, and links recollections and connotations together in strange and wonderful ways. A pause to gather our thoughts is not a sign of our decrepitude; it's a sign of the richness of our understanding. Also, scientific research shows that the more competently we *mentally* adapt to changing circumstances, the less rapidly we *physically* age. Adaptation requires relaxation. The more we honor ourselves as wise, experienced, and emotionally flexible, the younger we stay. Healthy aging is just one more way we come to understand the world more clearly and more deeply.

. . .

Sitting is the new smoking. Spending hours at a desk or computer is an act of self-destruction. Our circulatory, lymphatic, immune, and endocrine systems all require physical exercise to function properly, and the more we get, the better. Our bodies evolved to move, not to sit. By remaining stationary for too long, particularly on chairs, we interrupt the natural workings of our body, many of which occur beneath our conscious awareness. What's more, the air indoors is often polluted and full of mold, dust, and industrial pollutants. Set an alarm to remind you to get up, stretch, take a walk (outside if possible) every twenty minutes or so. Make it a habit, and you will live longer, suffer fewer afflictions, and have more energy, too.

. . .

Extreme exercise—indeed extremes of all kinds—is best left to entertainers. While very much in vogue in a culture that embraces risk and requires constant titillation, extreme exercise is incongruent with health and longevity. Despite generating short term pleasures, seeking thrills by flirting with injury and death reveals a numbed, desensitized state, completely contrary to a quiet, harmonious, awake, aware, and sensitive mind and body. Life-affirming pursuits such as swimming, traditional Asian martial arts, yoga, walking, or jogging are better long-term rectification options. Beyond that, or perhaps even better, how about vigorous sex with an enthusiastic partner?

. . .

Dependent upon artificial energy sources and confined in buildings that insulate us from both the elements and natural light, we lose touch with the circadian rhythms upon which a healthy body depends. If we cannot live in an unadulterated natural environment—and both the burgeoning need for sustainable agriculture and the communication options opened by the Internet make this more feasible than ever—at least we can make healthier lifestyle choices. Work when the sun is out and sleep under the moon's watchful eye. Slow down in winter, relax when it rains, and take advantage of brisk temperatures to exercise. These habits put us in better accord with natural cycles.

. . .

My teacher's teacher, Chen Quanzhong, seventeenth-generation teacher in his family's line, may be the greatest living practitioner of the martial art of tai chi ch'uan. In his nineties at the time of this writing, Great Grandmaster Chen lived through some of the toughest times in modern Chinese history, including the so-called Great Leap Forward (1958–1962), during which as many as fifty-five million people were murdered or starved to death. During the inaptly named Cultural Revolution, the Maoist government expropriated his factory and reduced his position there to that of floor-mopping janitor. Despite this, and at times nearly starving while raising seven children on a handful of dollars per week, he managed to lift his personal practice to dizzying heights. To this day, Great Grandmaster Chen strides about with the gait and the physique of a healthy, powerful, much-younger man, eclipsing his rivals in the martial arts and setting an example for us all.

Decades ago, I interviewed him for a leading martial arts magazine. One of the first questions I asked him was about cross-training, as exercise gurus and advocates then and now continue to advocate the practice.

"Cross-training?" he asked.

"Using weights, running, swimming, rowing, bicycling."

"Ah," he said, as I scribbled his response on my notepad. "Very, very important. Wonderful. Useful. Popular. Don't do it."

It took me a while to sort out that what he meant was that tai chi, being a Daoist practice, was all about creating connections inside the body. This is achieved by recruiting both stabilizer muscles and connective tissue so as to engage the entire body whenever any part is moved. Such connection also requires relaxing and sinking to embrace the effects of gravity, as opposed to fighting them in the way of a ballerina. He went on to explain that, once we learn to do so, we can bring that particular skill to bear during any activity. The emphasis, of course, was on creating the right mindset and physical attitude before doing external work.

Later, while critiquing my own practice, the great grandmaster reminded me that slow, correct, fully-relaxed tai chi is major isometric work and requires good nutritional support.

"Eat more beef," he suggested.

I couldn't bring myself to tell a man for whom beef was an almost unheard-of luxury that I was a vegetarian. I could not explain to someone who had experienced starvation that the world had changed, that the torture chambers we called factory farms were far more destructive than they are beneficial. I could not bring myself to tell him that I felt unnecessarily killing animals was morally wrong and that a balanced, plant-based diet was both ethical and healthy. Instead, I chose to take to heart the underlying message that if we want to achieve great things, we have to begin by taking great care of ourselves.

. . .

Thousands of years before the field of epigenetics was born, Daoism considered the environment's power to affect our mood, as well as the connection between mood and mental state. One of Daoism's key precepts is that, in order to reach an enlightened state of mind, we must have a strong body; with both we can weather life's most violent storms. No practice builds the body/mind—while simultaneously training us in conflict resolution—more perfectly than authentic, original tai chi ch'uan. Moving in natural spirals, cleaving to no plan, going with the flow, and embracing one's nature are the building blocks of the art, and are present in every movement. Tai chi is a path to both longevity and enlightenment.

. . .

Because we are complex biological and spiritual beings, we are
subject to the effects of countless, constantly shifting inner and
outer forces. Sensing the world around us with trained eyes,
ears, touch, and tongue, we can everywhere see *yin* and *yang*
in an intimate dance. The binary on-off position of switches
is what makes our digital world possible, for example, and the
gradual swap of winter and summer defines our yearly cycle.
While we might be tempted to focus on the simple duality
of this setup—the existence of opposites in all things and the
tension between them—it is actually the way the two opposites
change positions, like kings on a chess board defecting to the
other player's side, that defines this universal game. There is
no *yang* without *yin*, no *yin* without *yang*, and one is constantly
in the process of becoming the other. Thus, in noticing what
causes us stress and what helps us relax, who supports us in
our work to grow and improve and who holds us back, we can
create our own balance and move ourselves forward. There is a
yin and *yang* to relaxation, see, and one to rectification as well.
Embracing this truth, we can create harmonious lives filled
with compassion, wisdom, and awareness of resources.

· · ·

Dreams reveal important insights and truths, yet one of the
most pervasive plagues of our time is sleeplessness. People brag
about how little sleep they need, some even taking it as a badge
of honor or machismo to stumble blearily through the day or
rely on stimulants to function. Scientific research now shows
that sleeping less than nine hours per night costs us brain cells.
Sleep is the time when the brain's version of the lymphatic
system actually cleans brain tissue, removing (among other
toxins) the plaque associated with Alzheimer's Disease. Why
not reprioritize and spend less time pushing so hard and more
time in rejuvenating sleep? If we do, we'll live longer, enjoy our

lives more, be able to discover true relaxation, and have more
opportunity to contribute work of meaning and quality.

. . .

All creatures above a certain phylogenetic level need to sleep. This
means that once the nervous system develops a brain and reaches
a certain level of complexity, it shows the obvious yin/yang of
wakefulness and sleep. Daoist theory, which presaged binary theory,
thus applies directly to our state of consciousness. I'll call sleeping yin
and waking yang, because from a Daoist point of view, the former is
quiet and dark, and the latter is loud and bright. This same concept
applies to the rational versus the intuitive mind, as well as to the left
and right sides of the brain.

One of my students had a long term sleep problem. She tried
pharmaceutical sleep aids, aromatherapy, craniosacral therapy,
massage, exercise, professional talk therapy, anti-depressants, white
noise machines, and more—pretty much exhausting the gamut.
In a Daoist training session, we discussed the idea that her yang,
conscious, waking mind was somehow intruding on her yin, quiet,
sleeping mind, and rousing her repeatedly in the middle of the night
for no apparent reason.

I suggested that she might try to address what's bothering her. She
said there was nothing in her conscious mind that seemed an issue.
I asked about her work, family, relationships, health, finances—all
the usual suspects. She replied that, although no life was ever perfect,
she did not feel she had any big, pressing problems. All the same, I
could tell her yin and yang were not in balance, that something that
belonged on the yang side (wakefulness) had migrated over.

We practiced wuji meditation together as a solution. Standing quietly
under a large oak tree, a light, sub-tropical wind blowing and the

salty aroma of the nearby ocean enveloping us, we sank deeper and deeper into a relaxed state. I felt the energy flow up my spine and neck, over the top of my head, down the line of my nose, across the frenulum of my upper lip, and then turn in to meet the tip of my tongue where it rested on my hard palate, against the backside of my front teeth. From there, the energy traveled down my throat and followed the center line of my body. Visualizing that flow, feeling it, gave my mind something to do.

My focus was interrupted by the sound of my student weeping. I allowed her to feel what she needed to feel, to release her emotions without comment. After our session, she shared that her husband had taken a job in another city and was insisting they sell their house and move, something she had no wish to do. More discussion revealed her overall dissatisfaction with her marriage and other, deeper feelings of dissatisfaction with her life. Talking about them helped her decide on a course of action—confronting things rather than running from them, sharing her feelings rather than hiding them. Her meditation sessions grew more frequent after that, and she learned to go deeper and explore herself ably.

She started sleeping like a baby, too.

NOURISHING OURSELVES

How can we rectify a malnourished body? Contrary to popular opinion, a healthy diet need not be more expensive than an unhealthy one—it does require mindfulness, though, and careful selection of plant rather than animal protein sources. Historically speaking, human beings began to gain weight and get sick when we stopped preparing our meals from fresh and raw ingredients and came to rely on processed food. These days, agribusiness has trained us to accept fruits, vegetables, and grains packaged in plastic and transported long distances, sometimes thousands of miles. When we harvest directly from the garden rather than the package, we eliminate preservatives, additives, and genetic modifications that may have untoward consequences. The idea of growing local hasn't yet caught on big-time yet, but it must. New, small-scale agricultural technologies such as hydroponic tanks and computer-controlled plant nutrition, lighting, and watering, now make it possible for us to grow food in new ways and in places never considered suitable for farming before—vertically, in urban warehouses, for example, and in converted office buildings, patios, and small, green spaces. Growing our own vegetables, fruits, and herbs can be anything from a fun, healthy, and satisfying hobby to a small business. So can growing and harvesting certain species of seaweed, which are increasingly recognized as important, sustainable, and viable food sources. Such enterprises can save us money, improve our health, and conserve energy. Too, complementary growing strategies—you grow corn, I'll do tomatoes—unite communities. Let's all join the movement and grow!

. . .

A plant-based (vegan) diet is now the only environmentally sustainable option we have, and it lends us the mental clarity for our self-cultivation, too. Most people greatly misunderstand veganism, believing it to represent a paucity of choices; in fact, it is a far richer and more varied diet than any meat eater can embrace. Eliminating meat, poultry, eggs, dairy, and fish, a mere five-ingredient group, leaves us with a vast array of foodstuffs. Plant-based eating is a creative and marvelous lifestyle embraced by millions around the world. Paired with the elimination of refined sugar, it is also nutritious and enjoyable, and counters many degenerative diseases, including dairy-fueled cancers and the malignant effects of pesticides and hormones concentrated in meat. As if that were not enough—and, of course, it is—veganism also encourages foraging, a growing trend in rural areas and an opportunity to both spend more time in the woods and to learn about the nutritional value of local plants. Last, but by no means least, when we choose not to eat animals, we make a stand against wholesale cruelty and institutional torture. Veganism represents an awakening of compassion. Those who still eat animal products often resist admitting they are harming themselves, and live in denial about needlessly causing suffering. Let's all try this diet, despite our varying protein needs, preferences, and genetics. Even if we need supplements such as vitamin B12 to make it complete, most of us can make it work.

· · ·

Dairy products are morbidly unhealthy. How appealing would it be to put your lips to a cow's teat? Yet, a maleficent industry drives our appetite for milk, cream, butter, cheese, yoghurt, and dairy desserts, convincing us in a ubiquitous, daily, high-budget blitz that the secretion of an animal species evolutionarily and phylogenetically distant from our own is essential for our well-being. Dairy-industry-funded studies on the necessity of milk for bone density and calcium color the way even nutritionists see the role of dairy, while millions suffer from calcified arteries, lactose intolerance, joint and auto-immune diseases, and obesity, all to keep Big Dairy rolling in profits. As if all of this were not enough, the life of a dairy cow, trapped, penned, artificially fattened, injected with antibiotics, and milked, is a fate far worse than death. Add the looming human health crisis associated with antibiotic-resistant organisms, killing more of us every day as a result of consuming so many drug-tainted foods, and we have a real house of horrors. Let's boycott dairy products and eliminate these poisons from our diets.

. . .

It is believed that sugar cane was cultivated back in New Guinea in Neolithic times. When European explorers came across sugar, they brought it back to their native lands as an intoxicant, as a sculpture medium, and as medicine. Nobles of the European courts carried it around in little boxes and used just a pinch—like snuff or cocaine—for the rush of taste and energy. Now sugar is in absolutely everything, from our bread to our cold cuts. Yes, that's right, it's in our hotdogs. Don't believe it? Take a look at some labels. It has proven to be the most dangerous plant we have ever domesticated and has given birth to one of the most pernicious industries Planet Earth has ever seen. Not only is it a dirty and destructive crop in the sub-tropics and tropics, evidence points to sugar's links to cancer, obesity, diabetes, and, most recently, Alzheimer's Disease. Make a life-saving change and beat the Big Sugar lobby at the same time: boycott any and all products containing added sugar. Not buzzing from sugar all the time, we can begin to relax.

The role of the so-called "bonesetter" in China is sometimes compared to that of the chiropractor in the Western traditions. It is actually different, and arguably more important. The advent of regional hospitals is a recent one in China, a country so vast and lacking in infrastructure that, even today, large swaths of the population do not have reliable access to modern medical care. For millennia, village healers were the only medical resource for rural populations. Because these individuals might see anything from diabetes, venereal disease, amputated limbs, anaphylactic shock, cancer, heart disease, breach births, to skin lesions, they were trained to offer a wide range of medical services. They couldn't cure everything, of course, but then neither can even the best doctors in our own cutting-edge hospitals.

During one of my frequent visits to the south of China, I went with my tai chi master to rural Guangning county in Guangdong province. Traveling with us were a few of my master's other students, and a few of my own as well. The purpose of the trip was to visit a relative of my master, the latest in a line of bonesetters, stretching back many hundreds of years. Some healing lineages are noted for herbal potions, and others for treating chronic diseases such as asthma or ulcers. My teacher's family is known for being good at literally setting broken bones.

The family clinic was a modest four-room affair located in an older building on the outskirts of a small village. It was equipped with a rudimentary x-ray machine and some triage tools distributed between two treatment rooms. Nearby, the town mayor had recently invested in a series of townhouses that looked like they belonged in Beverly Hills. Because we were honored foreign guests, the mayor gave us one of these townhouses to use during our stay. I was astonished by the marble floors, the Western toilets, the chandeliers, granite countertops, and modern appliances.

On the second day of our visit, while having wonderful Bamboo County Clean Scent Green Tea served to us in traditional fashion, a sixteen-year-old boy was ushered into the clinic. He had just suffered from a motorbike accident. He was sweating and pale, and his arm was dangling at his side. Bones protruded from his arm, clear evidence of compound fractures. The bonesetter immediately inserted a few acupuncture needles. The moment they were in, the boy stopped trembling, and his breathing slowed. Relaxed, he thanked the bonesetter for stopping his pain. At that point, the bonesetter sat with the boy's arm in his lap and began to play his fingertips up and down *along the boy's arm as if it were a musical instrument. I asked my master what he was doing.*

"Feeling the bones, of course."

"I'd like to see an x-ray," interrupted another of my master's students, a medical doctor from Florida.

The bonesetter smiled, said an x-ray wasn't necessary, but agreed to do one anyway.

The picture showed not only compound fractures but a myriad of other smaller cracks, with numerous bits of bone floating about. The boy hadn't merely fallen off his bike; a car or truck had run over his arm, crushing it.

"Big surgery," my doctor friend said. "Lots of pins. Long recovery. That arm will never be the same."

The bonesetter jiggled the acupuncture needles and returned to work. He continued working the boy's flesh, pressing here, pulling there, his eyes closed, his concentration trancelike. We all watched silently as the protruding bones, lightly swabbed with antiseptic, slipped back into place. After half an hour, the arm appeared normal. A lot of the initial puffiness was gone and the patient was obviously far more comfortable. The bonesetter wrapped the arm in gauze and then applied a mustard-colored plaster. He then gave the boy extensive instructions, which my master translated.

"This plaster cast will not dry but will seep into the bones through the skin and help them heal. After three days, the boy is to take it off and rewrap it with fresh bandages and the second bag of herbs, which will dry harder and keep everything in place as it heals. There is a third bag of plaster for him to use in a final cast for an additional two weeks."

"A wet cast," the Florida doctor muttered. "How can that work? I'd like to see another x-ray."

Again, the bonesetter willingly led the boy to the x-ray machine. When we examined the images of his work, we were all stunned. The bones were so perfectly aligned that only the faintest lines revealed the breaks. We compared the before and after films. Even the small fragments of bone had been eased back into place.

"This puts anything we can do to shame," my doctor friend declared. "We'd have used pins, general anesthesia, antibiotics, sutures, and more. And to think, this is a vanishing art."

"One of many," my master said sadly.

Greed rather than compassion has become the primary motivator in our health care system. Physicians and other healthcare providers must remember they are in service, not in business. They deserve our respect, and often our gratitude, but not mansions and yachts. They are primarily mechanics whom we pay to fix what is broken, and in most countries, are treated as such. How were they crowned the High Priests of American Society and who thinks they should be? Their own lobby, that's who. Adversarial, lordly, and condescending phrases such as "against medical advice," "patient compliance," and "take as directed" have no place in the cooperative dance that medical care must become. Commanding rather than convincing patients, physicians who use such words appear more interested in power and profit than healing, more driven by ego than humanity. Medical care is a right. It must be a mandate of government and community. Assuming the leading role in fostering our own good health, rather than relying primarily on others to do so for us, is a key step in rectifying our body/mind. A healthy lifestyle and a self-reliant attitude are our best hedges against the degenerative diseases associated with aging. We have the right for our physician's undivided attention during an office visit, and to leave that visit with our questions answered. Let's remind our insurance agents and healthcare providers—kindly but firmly—that we are the customers, and the customer is king.

. . .

At one time or another, the body will inevitably sicken. Health and sickness are the *yin* and *yang* of the cycle of living. Think of this cycle as represented by a sine wave. What we want for the relaxed and rectified body is a low frequency (sickness doesn't happen too often) and a low amplitude (when we do get sick, it is not too serious). When we sicken, we must turn to one another for assistance, not to some elaborate and concocted system. In the aboriginal experience, healthcare meant caring for the sick. Shamans used rituals and hallucinogens to travel to other dimensions and address the root cause of illness or disease, facing down monsters and paying karmic debt in order to bring a patient back to health. These days, the process of healthcare has become a tub of pork, curated primarily by Big Insurance and secondarily by Big Pharma. How did we let a corporate function that profits from our fear of life's twists and turns come to rule the way we are treated when we're sick? How did rolling the dice on future events become an industry full of fat cats with private jets? How did protecting people from misfortune become a for-profit enterprise at all? How did it become acceptable to profit from medications or medicines? In the Daoist view, services like healthcare are the responsibility of leadership; it is our job to take care of each other in times of misfortune, not to benefit from suffering and misery. Controls on healthcare are more urgently needed than perhaps in any other industry. The notion of a profitable

hospital is an abomination. Until we obviate the need for
health insurance by mandating universal healthcare, we must
legislate not-for-profit status for insurance carriers and bring
tight price controls to bear upon devices, procedures, and
medications. Big Pharma should be forced to justify the cost
of its products in the same way it proves safety and efficacy.
Let's vote out of office any government representative who
either acts as a lobbyist for the pharmaceutical industry or is
beholden to that industry in any way. Let's create a shift in the
culture, and the system, through talking loudly and frankly
about unreasonable profits and costs. Isn't it time to put people
before profit?

...

The shameful cabal between Big Pharma, health insurance
companies, lobbyists, and the American Medical Association
has worked hard to discredit healthcare modalities not under
its control. If people stopped taking pills in favor of tai chi,
yoga, or meditation, for example, billions of dollars in profits
would vanish. While there are many miraculous aspects to
Western medicine, its most impressive dimension may be
its profitability. Actually *curing* widespread diseases would
deprive our healthcare system of the vast profits to be had in
keeping us in treatment, keeping us popping pills and making
office visits, buying insurance and going for tests. This is the
fox guarding the henhouse on a high-stakes farm. What can
we do? Well, while alternative care is only rarely and lightly
reimbursed by insurance, we are nonetheless free to explore
the world of nutraceuticals, Ayurveda, and Traditional Chinese
Medicine. The last, a construct of the Chinese government,
is a simplified, gelded, and comparatively weak amalgam of a
rich and startlingly effective mosaic of thousands of healing
traditions. All the same, acupuncture works, and so does herbal

medicine. All that is required of us is an open mind and a bit of patience, as many of these modalities require some time and diligence, on the part of both patient and caregiver, to work their magic.

. . .

Touch is not only one of our most exquisite senses, it is one of human life's necessities. Living creatures from brine shrimp and sea sponges to pangolins and gorillas understand this, and may variously aggregate, bump, intertwine, rub, and caress each other. Through a long period of devolution, moving through religious proscriptions to the rising primacy of our virtual worlds, many people suffer daily from a lack of human touch. What say we break the barriers of political correctness and ask for a hug when we need one? If we can't afford a professional massage, why not barter for touch, offer a foot, neck, or shoulder rub in return for the same? Imagine how much tension can be harmlessly released this way, how many frustrations and misunderstandings avoided. Touch is natural.

A SENSE OF SELF

Our worldview is learned; we are not born with it. Our preconceptions, joys, irritations, and feelings of what is and what should be—all these are taught to us by others. It is certainly easiest to simply accept what we're given, yet when the model passed down to us tires, sickens, or depresses us, or when it leaves us hungry for more, for something ineffable, something we can't quite seem to touch, a change may be in order. Rather than the negative, angry, frustrated, nihilistic, and ultimately violent way many people live now, what say we make a deliberate effort to relax, to breathe, to close our eyes, and to scan our body from top to bottom for tension, deliberately releasing what we find? This takes practice, dedication, and a bit of initial discipline, but it soon becomes a habit and is not very hard. After all, if we learned to be tense, we can learn to be relaxed. We can learn to evaluate and discard what doesn't strengthen our equilibrium and appreciate and embrace whatever does. In the end, assuming a more relaxed position to life's unfolding is just about willing ourselves to see things differently, to cultivate a transcendent feeling of love for the flow of nature and the welfare of all living beings. A significant side benefit of relaxing this way is that it opens us to a sense of gratitude and wonder, and allows our lives to feel more fulfilling, important, and meaningful.

. . .

Our popular culture emphasizes and rewards winning the rat race and taking care of #1. While self-cultivation with an eye to creating a clear, calm, and stable mind is of paramount importance, self-centeredness and selfishness are not. Taking care of ourselves, indeed rewarding and defining ourselves, can often mean taking care of those closest to us. Altruism is in our genes and has been shown to be essential to our survival, so why not volunteer for the benefit of people we do not know at all? Broadening our horizons and our efforts this way can bring a myriad of unforeseen blessings, including great health advantages. A rectified and relaxed body/mind is ready for this kind of behavior, and indeed welcomes it.

. . .

Zhuangzi, the butterfly dreamer, based his teachings on Laozi's philosophy, but he was a literary genius in his own right. His sense of self, humor, and society has endeared him to readers, Daoist adepts, and schoolchildren for more than two thousand years. He worked as a clerk in the town of Meng, in the state of Song, before China became a nation. Though married, he lived as a recluse, choosing poverty out of a desire for a simple life, and preferring rural surroundings so as to be close to nature. What more we know about him comes from his own writings, and from a few stories about him.

In one of these, Zhuangzi is peacefully fishing with a bamboo pole along the Pu River, when a couple of government functionaries from the nearby state of Ch'u approach him with a document from their prince that names him prime minister. The officials stress that their ruler has heard of Zhuangzi's wisdom and is in need of his counsel. The officials remind him he is a beggar living in a hovel and that the offer is not only an honor but a path to far better circumstances.

Zhuangzi stares at the river and takes his time answering. At last, he declares he has heard of a turtle with auspicious markings on its shell that had been killed and turned into an object of worship in a temple shrine. "Do you suppose the turtle is happier famous but stuffed, or alive and dragging its tail through the mud?" he asks the officials.

The men concede that, as far as the turtle is concerned, it is doubtless better to be alive in the mud than dead in the temple. "Exactly," Zhuangzi answers. "So, go home and leave me to drag my tail through the mud."

The point of the story, of course, is that Zhuangzi's values, indeed his entire life, serve as an example of the quintessentially pure Daoist, the lover of nature who cares nothing about what others think of him and has no interest in the affairs of men, however seductive their trappings may be. In his view, it is a far higher and nobler thing to live an authentic life, pursuing internal development and learning from nature, than to become embroiled in what the Abrahamic tradition might consider to be an idolatrous career.

Embracing our true nature rather than falsehoods, we have learned, is what rectification really means, even when the purity of our personal path makes us loners and nonconformists. Zhuangzi accepted things as they really are, reveled in the way of nature as a comfort and a source of joy, and avoided rebelling collectively because he understood that to push back against something is to be controlled by it just as surely as is conforming to it. He knew that cleaving to organizational structures is antithetical to Dao.

...

Behold the turtle, who makes progress only when he sticks his neck out. To stay in our comfort zone is to be ruled by fear. Fearful, we shrink inexorably into death rather than expand confidently into life. Move forward with consideration, in a relaxed fashion, and with an eye towards what is most important. Don't believe negative talk. Accept no internally-generated limitations and, while you're at it, donate to turtle conservation projects. There is a reason so very many cultures depict turtles as supporting the world. These creatures are the quintessence of steadfastness, patience, and endurance. They have survived hundreds of millions of years, but just a few short decades of exploitation by human beings have led them to suffer the dubious distinction of being the most highly endangered group of vertebrates on Earth.

...

Reality may be no more than a glorified film emulsion, each frame being the present moment divided from the next by a dark strip of nothingness. In this darkness, all is created anew.

On and off we blink, in and out of existence. If the brightness of being is the *yang* of everyday life; the dark strip is the still and quiet place we call *wuji*, wherein everything is about to happen but hasn't yet. This dark strip is precisely the space within which we can reframe and recreate the thousands of versions of ourselves that live inside our heads, each the result of our memories, experiences, and moods, and the outside forces acting upon us. This reinvention represents a fantastic opportunity for rectification. In meditation or contemplation, we can play with this superpower, fixing all that we think is wrong and making it right. Since each frame stands apart from the one before and after, we can reinvent ourselves as often as we like without constraint. In traditional Western religious lingo, the *via affirmativa* now becomes the path of daily practice or devotion and the *via negativa* becomes the sudden reframing of our life and identity in the dark strips between the bright moments of our lives.

...

The gap between the way life is and the way we would like it to be creates what psychologists call cognitive dissonance, where the gap between our actions and beliefs creates disharmony. In the face of disharmony, relaxation disappears, stress manifests, our immune systems struggle, and our bodies collapse. We suffer hypertension, anxiety, insomnia, mood-swings, and more serious problems, too. Unable to find *wuji*, we cannot relax. Unable to relax, we cannot rectify ourselves. The price tag for forgetting that this too shall pass, for engaging this confusion and indulging in an attachment to the way we want things to be rather than appreciating how they are, is incredibly stiff and unfortunately widespread. We must fight the urge for instant gratification. One good technique to do this is substitution. Feeling the urge to gamble, we fold some origami instead; wanting to eat but knowing we're not really hungry, we drink a tall glass of water; seized by the need to check in with social media, we pick up the phone and call a friend; wanting to buy something, we add it to our "wish list," not our shopping cart. Such prescriptions for health, sanity, and a better world are really quite simple.

...

It is the absolute opposite of rectification to be self-involved. Without the contrast and context of our interactions with others, rectification is not only pointless, it is impossible. Despite this, many spiritual manuals cite the need to be kind to others on account of how such behavior will benefit us. How utterly cynical this is! How selfish and self-defeating. "Enlightened self-interest" is not only an offensive phrase, it is an oxymoronic characteristic of our "it's all about me" culture. We must not be kind to others because we think it will get us some kind of reward. We must not be altruistic because we think it benefits our personal genome. We must not be kind to others because we figure that, in the long term, our actions will come back to benefit us through financial gain, position, leverage, or opportunity. We must cultivate ourselves in order to become enlightened, not because it is enlightened to cultivate ourselves. Once enlightenment is achieved, all sense of "I" disappears and the independent self is recognized for the illusion it truly is. On the path to this state of freedom and perspective, we acknowledge that certain work must be done, namely living in service of other sentient beings. Watching such beings with a sense of compassion, we experience the odd and paradoxical sensation of feeling more love and closeness to them as our distance from them inevitably grows in proportion to our perspective.

...

It is better to be kind than it is to be accurate, even if one is
a drone pilot or nuclear engineer. This is because accuracy,
while enhancing effectiveness when our aim is true, does not
guarantee that we are aiming at the right thing. Kindness, by
contrast, assures our efforts are pointed in the right direction.
Striving for accuracy merely improves our personal focus,
while striving to be kind goes far beyond the individual and
affects the larger world. When exercising kindness, we notice a
rush of relaxing warmth right away.

...

As much as we would like to, it is not possible to live
completely without judging. The problem is that when we
judge, we grow tense. When tense, relaxation fades away and
we are left in a reactive mode that also blocks our efforts at
rectification. It is time to realize that judging is not only bad
for those whom we judge but also antithetical to our efforts at
self-improvement; the first step to putting our world back in
order is to refrain from judging. Taking this stance is the first
step to being wise enough to cultivate the difference between
discernment and judgment, that is, between recognizing
something for what it is and leaping to a conclusion based on
our own prejudices and limitations.

TIME AND ENERGY

If something feels wrong, it probably is. Intuition often senses
underlying patterns, tendencies, and trends long before logic
can find them. That's because it arises spontaneously from

relaxation, not from agendas, timetables, and pressures. Sourced from a different portion of the brain than the one that gives us logic, intuition can present as a gut feeling, as mysticism, insights, or transcendence. When our rational brain stands in opposition to our feelings and inclinations, balance is lost and with it the full experience of life as a human being. Thusly unbalanced, we are proverbial hamsters on wheels, spinning breathlessly while going nowhere in a blind, exhausting, and pointless hurry. Both reason and intuition are needed. Rectification means bringing the two assets into balance.

. . .

Why not intuit a number for the days of life we have left? Why feel a reason to make that number a reasonable one? Let's not think too hard about it; let's just go with the first number that pops up. Daoists rely on intuition, remember? Whatever the number may be, a handful, or many, many thousands, let us fill those days mindful of the fact that, with each one that passes, there is one less left. Let's make a random, unique, unbridled, creative, and unconventional job of each of those days, and thereby embrace the crazy chaos of our very own natures. This is the way forward to a higher version of ourselves.

. . .

There is a fascinating interaction between the Daoist emphasis on the concept of *wuji*, heat, and the perception of the passage of time. Standard concepts of time see it as moving forward in linear fashion. Linear movement requires heat. In absolute cold, where nothing moves, we cannot say change is happening or time is passing. This state of emptiness, pregnant with infinite possibility, is the state we hope to achieve through

certain types of meditation. It simulates that period in creation
before anything was moving, before there was any heat (or
impulses, desires, or fears). It therefore stands to reason that if
we can achieve such a state, we can come to a timeless place.
This could mean a slowing of aging. It might also give us the
mental space not to pull the trigger, not to shout, not to curse,
not to commit when it's wrong to do so, not to fail to commit
when to do so is right and necessary. It gives us space to make
the behavioral changes we wish to and to come to the deeper
understanding of life we seek. Free of heat, motion, and time,
we are, paradoxically, immortal.

· · ·

Time is our most precious resource. It is finite and cannot be
renewed. Unfortunately, we are wont to squander it and, even
worse, to trade it for a concocted, non-renewable resource
called money. While the so-called "mindfulness movement"
represents the commercialization of spirituality, the principles
on which the movement is based can indeed help us savor the
passage of time in a meaningful way. Let's stop wasting time
on projects and pursuits of no true benefit to others or to
ourselves. Each moment of pleasure or pain deserves our pure
attention. After all, each moment is unique, arrives precisely
on schedule and will never be seen again. Let's forego our
addiction to setting appointments and filling empty days when
we are lucky enough to have them. Let's notice what our minds
do when our wristwatch or smartphone does not tell us we
have to be somewhere or do something this moment. Let's end
time's tyranny and savor it instead.

· · ·

Constructing a sense of self based on the vicissitudes and vagaries of social media is like using tissue-paper bricks to build a house. There are no people on social media; there are only electronic doppelgangers. Trying to either one-up or sympathize is no way to relax. Nobody really looks like his or her photo, nobody's life is neither so fabulous nor so miserable as they portray. This is not because we're all liars— although most of us fiddle with the facts when posting—but because there is simply a poor correlation between life in three dimensions and life in a two-dimensional screen. In assembling our day-to-day moods, plans, and goals, we are far better off using feedback from those we can see and touch and hear and smell than relying on that which glows so seductively at night when we are alone. Let's limit our exposure to damaging stimuli by tuning out the digital world and tuning into each other. Human beings are always strongest, inside and out, when we work together in real space and time.

Long before I found a real teacher, I read volume after volume on Eastern mysticism, all of which used the words qi *or* prana *to describe a life force that may also be translated as circulation or breath. I learned that this force flows through prescribed channels, that we can direct it with our intention, that we're born with it, and that we can augment it by meditating, breathing correctly, and eating right. I also came to understand that its absence means death, its presence means life, and that all living things (and, in some Chinese traditions, even inanimate natural objects like rocks and rivers) are imbued with it. I discovered that its quality can be improved by certain body/mind practices, and that it can be diminished by fatigue, illness, or stress. Later, I was told that, in China, it is not uncommon to say to a person, "Your* qi *looks good today," and that Daoist medicine is based on* qi *manipulation.*

*I claimed to accept the existence of this energy and often cited it
when chatting with friends, but deep down I wondered whether it
really existed as a discrete entity. I suspected it might be simply a
primitive term for the circulation of the blood, the tingling of nerves,
ultrasound, infrared, a soft-tissue-specific communication system,
the flow of lymph, or, more technically, the bioelectric energy of life
stimulated by the charge potential that exists across cell membranes.
I was, in short, on an intellectual mission to convince myself qi/
prana was real.*

*I can't say I did a very good job. There was all this literature, yes, but
there were precious few scientific studies, the sort of double-blind,
placebo-controlled stuff of which Western academic careers are made
and from which Western minds draw definitive conclusions. What
I found was hearsay, anecdotes, passionate pledges, affirmations,
mumbo-jumbo, and the occasional wise nod and heavy-lidded wink.
All that, I'm sorry to say, did not sway me. I was too much a product
of my Western education.*

*Things did not get much more definitive or clear when I finally got
down to the business of a body/mind practice. I did yoga diligently
during college, and started martial arts immediately thereafter, but
when everyone spoke of feeling a cotton ball of energy pulsing in
their hands or an electric current rising up their spines, I wondered
whether there might be something wrong with me because I didn't
feel any of that at all. I ameliorated my frustration by telling myself
I wasn't far enough along the path of training to feel such things but
that at some point in the future I, too, would feel the energy of life.*

*I could never be mistaken for a quick study. It took me decades to
realize I was barking up the wrong tree. I was looking to learn more
and more and more, when in fact it was unlearning I required. Put
another way, an awareness of life's pulsing energy (plus sensitivity
to a myriad of other inputs) had been available all along. I needed*

only to disable the nearly ubiquitous mental filters I discuss elsewhere in this book. I had made what I now feel is the cardinal mistake of modern, technological society: I had let my logical mind overwhelm my awareness to the point where I denied very real sensorial input.

We don't live in a culture that exalts the intuitive mind the way some Eastern cultures do. That emphasis on reason at the expense of reliance on subconscious knowing has led us to the moon and cured many diseases but has gotten in the way when it comes to tasting the subtleties of life, the energy of body/mind practices, and even the true depth of love. It turns out that if we wish to sweeten and deepen our everyday experience with new insights and sensations, we must set aside much of what we've been taught in school, read in books, and learned from our parents. It's tough to do this, because even though the rational, profit-based Western worldview now threatens our very existence, it distracts us from ourselves and nature. The price of this distraction is an inability to sense the subtle cycles and energies of our lives. This is disastrous; those cycles offer beauty, insight and answers, too.

Researchers all over the world are substantiating, qualifying and quantifying so-called "supernatural phenomena" like qi. In the meantime, however, all we really need to do to experience them is to pay attention during quiet times. Listen to our bodies just before we fall asleep or create our own quiet through our focused attention anywhere, anytime. The anticipatory tingle we feel in a social situation? That's energy. The way we're unaccountably drawn to a stranger, or repelled by one? That's energy, too. The realization that creeps up on us that the tiger in that gorgeous new zoo enclosure is desperately yearning to be free, that's us sensing energy, as is the awareness that the plant in the office needs water, the creepy suspicion that someone died badly in the house the realtor is showing us, the knowledge that we need to call our kid, or the feeling someone is creeping up on us in a dark alley.

All we have to do is suspend judgment and we'll feel life's energy right away. It's everywhere.

Authenticity is no boon to corporate interests and no prized asset of the greedy. Rather, like progressive thinking and true and spontaneous action, authenticity threatens existing power bases, rattles the cage of the complacent and self-satisfied, and is a bee in the bonnet of hoodwinkers everywhere. Let's be authentic in everything we say and do. Pretending or prevaricating, we become obsessed with remembering all the lies we told. How can we possibly relax under such circumstances? How can we possibly expend energy in rectifying ourselves, in building new and better versions of who we are, if our attention is commanded by pretense and deception? Being true, in all senses of the word, is a prerequisite to the work that is the focus of this chapter.

. . .

One of the most obvious social contracts we have is to tell the truth to ourselves and to each other. Yet our system of laws and government discourages us from doing so. In a dog-eat-dog capitalistic society, wherein competition rules instead of cooperation, the truth often puts us at a disadvantage. Tell the truth to the police and we go to jail, tell the truth to attorneys and we get sued, tell the truth to our boss and we get fired. Often, it is not the facts that prove to be to our disadvantage but rather their recounting. The mere fact that we would be willing to tell the truth can make us appear a rube waiting to be taken advantage of by others. What a strange business this is! What say we start lauding truth tellers, embracing personal honesty, celebrating the courage it takes to be who we are, and stigmatizing gaming and deception in the way we now do honesty? What say we start a campaign of frankness about our strengths and weaknesses, and what we really want and care about? If rectification is about anything, it's about being honest and clear with ourselves and others.

. . .

What a miraculous world we will have when everyone focuses on being great inside rather than proving their worth outside. The notions of efficiency and effectiveness in the context of "getting things done" is one of the great diseases of our time. How can we relax and rectify ourselves if our attention is constantly pointing outward? Remember, the work assigned to us by others is rarely intended to benefit us. To be satisfied and content with the work we do within ourselves, however, is to find joy in beating our inner demons rather than keeping up with our neighbor. If we listen to the songs of our souls and dance to them, the surprising and delightful miracles that erupt will help us relax and set us on the path to becoming heroes. This is what rectification means, and it is a fine recipe for happiness and enlightenment.

. . .

Before undertaking any new regimen or routine, particularly when we know we are going to judge its value based on the results we see, it is important to accurately assess our starting point. An objective measure of our progress, not to mention understanding where we've ended up, depends entirely upon knowing at what point, and with what advantages or handicaps, we entered the game. The loss of twenty pounds, for example, can be a substantial achievement for someone who weighs 180, less so for someone who is morbidly obese at 650. As we work to relax and rectify and realize our goals, hopes, and ambitions, what say we be frank, kind, firm, and gentle about the obstacles we face in achieving our goals?

. . .

Why are so very many of us willing to accept the so-called rat race as the model for our lives? Why would we agree to push as hard as we can to get ahead of others, exhausting ourselves in the process? The only ones we are serving when we push, push, push, work, work, work, are the vampires subsisting off our efforts and shysters who wish to sell us things. Wisdom prizes efficiency and effectiveness over exhausting labor. Let's relax and rectify ourselves instead. Let's eat when we are hungry (but not when we aren't) and sleep when we are tired. Rising in social class and financial position often comes at the cost of indentured servitude to corporations and small business concerns. Let's rebel against this model, find a way to live that does not paralyze our options so. Let's embrace *wu wei* (effortless action). As psychologist Albert Ellis suggested, let's stop "should-ing" on ourselves.

. . .

Multitasking is the sign of a stressed and diseased mind simultaneously doing many things poorly. Quality work, quality thinking, and a healthy body all require quiet focus. Only with mental quiet, and its attendant low rates of heartbeat and respiration, can we disappear into our creative endeavors to benefit ourselves and the world around us.

. . .

Why settle for anything in life that does not awaken us and gratify all our senses while we work for the betterment of the world? Once we have food, shelter, and companionship, why engage in any other relationship, work, project, or pastime that does not completely and totally engage, involve, and reward us? If we are only here once and this life is all there is, isn't it time to stop listening to media messages about who we should be and instead concentrate on who we actually are? Why pursue goals that benefit no one and fail to stir and ignite us? Isn't it time to find the virtually limitless energy available in our passions? Rectification leads to this kind of focus and prioritization.

. . .

As a young man, I was an ardent motorcyclist. It wasn't so much the need to thumb my nose at prudence and convention that led me to ride (although that was certainly part of it!), nor was it an addiction to the thrill of twisting the throttle or tilting the horizon through turns. Rather, I grew addicted to the feeling of being out in a world where the scenery was constantly around me and changing. I felt like a bird flying low across the landscape. There was no cage of steel and glass around me and I could change direction at will. A point of interest on the horizon was enough to compel me, and I had the means to bring myself to it with little effort. In short, motorcycling was a medium of immediate physical gratification.

It was also an adventure. I traveled the country on two wheels, meeting people, stopping to write screenplays and books on a laptop computer in parks and cafés. Sometimes I had a destination. Other times, I packed toiletries and a few changes of clothes in my saddlebags, pointed my front wheel toward one compass point or other, and set out. I was always relieved to shed the material constraints of being a renter or householder behind, always delighted to bid adieu to possessions that could, if I was not careful, define me. I had not yet become a father, nor committed myself to service as a monk, and the risk/benefit analysis of riding still worked in favor of a life spent at least partially on two wheels.

One year, a magazine ad for an antique bike caught my fancy. I traveled to Maryland, bought it, strapped my bags across the seat, and headed west to California. The machine didn't really have enough power for highway cruising—rarely a motorcyclist's choice of route anyway—and so I puttered along secondary roads known as 'blue highways' for their color in travel guides and on maps. I traveled only by day—the bike's headlight did little to illuminate the road—and always at a modest pace, as its suspension and brakes were not designed for spirited riding. Despite its limitations, I loved the bike's simplicity, build quality, vintage look, stone-axe reliability, and soothing engine note, too.

I had in mind to have a look at Eureka Springs, Arkansas. I'd heard it was a lovely place. A few hours east of town, riding atop a levee bisecting a reservoir, I felt like a motorized eagle skimming the surface and scanning for signs of a meal below the surface. I noticed storm clouds behind the trees at the edge of the water. Within a very few minutes, rain began to fall.

In what seemed like an impossibly short time, the sky turned black and I was riding through a deluge. The reservoir level quickly rose, and water began to slosh over the road. I noticed a couple of eighteen-wheelers in my rearview mirror and found myself behind a third. Sandwiched between the giant trucks, I feared they wouldn't see me in the heavy rain. The air turned to soup. My face shield fogged and I had trouble seeing where I was going. I had no choice but to continue. The road had no shoulder.

The rooster-tail from the truck tires in front of me slapped me hard enough to jerk my head. The water reached axle level, rendering my old-style drum brakes inoperative. My foot pegs disappeared under water. The rain penetrated my jacket at the wrists and neck. A cold trickle made its way down my chest and down my back, too. I pulled the brake lever regularly to remind the truck behind me that I was still there, but I doubted the brake light was bright enough for him to see. I was cold, worried, and miserable, and those feelings only intensified as the storm did the same.

And then, from the depths of fear and despair, I was suddenly seized by the desire to sing. I belted out my favorite rock-and-roll tunes and did my best to conjure Broadway hits my mother used to croon when I was a kid. Barely able to see, in mortal danger of losing control or of being run over, wet and shivering, I had the sudden realization that I was on a vintage bike, crossing the country, literally immersed in nature, and having a great adventure. My mood shifted. I licked the rainwater from my lips. I grinned from ear to ear.

I made it safely to town, had perhaps the most delicious cup of coffee of my life, spent a few hours in a laundromat getting everything clean and dry, serviced my bike, and learned a valuable lesson about perception, attitude, gratitude, and being in the moment.

These days, I engage mindful awareness at every opportunity. And when it rains, I seek shelter from which to enjoy it, particularly if there is lightning and thunder.

. . .

One good working definition of self-cultivation is becoming free from the shackles that bind us. Of the various prisons we choose—an overly material life, a bad partnership, a dead-end career, soul-crushing work—none is nearly so good at diminishing us as our own imagination is. We can rectify ourselves while in a state or federal prison, but not in one we have erected between our ears. It is such a bittersweet irony

that the very thing that can set us free can also, in the form
of fear, be our most potent adversary. In our meditations, we
must address our fears squarely and without delay, beginning
with mere anxiety and progressing to paranoia and flat-out
terror. Repeating supportive, positive, and reprogramming
messages to ourselves during meditation is one technique.
Another is visualization, wherein we see ourselves around
the people or inside the situations that cause us distress and
actively change how we behave in the "screenplay" for the
movie we're watching behind our eyes. Qualified meditation
teachers can offer myriad other techniques. Only when
we have calmed our minds and seen our fear as merely a
construct of our own devising can we begin the deeper work of
expanding consciousness.

CHAPTER TWO

REBALANCING DAILY LIFE

Having achieved a relaxed and rectified body/mind, the next step in our quest for global healing is to carefully consider our daily routine. This means examining our priorities in the light of how they drive our decisions, looking critically at the way we spend our time, observing the degree to which we engage the world around us as opposed to retreat from it, and evaluating the causes and people we spiritually and materially support.

This rebalancing is still part of self-cultivation. There are no cardinal sins here, but there are plenty of ways to stray from the path. The most common one is to constantly sample delicious new items from available spiritual offerings without ever making a meal of any of them. We can become addicted to new ideas just as easily as to any mind-altering substance; we can fall into the trap of constant intellectual titillation at the expense of deep thinking and mastery of ourselves. There are, after all, so very many shopping-mall gurus selling gimmicks and gadgets and games to change our lives, so many community-center teachers who have climbed Mt. Everest, so many yoginis who have gone to stretch in India and can rivet us with their contortions, and so many books offering recipes for peace, prosperity, power, and prestige. No wonder we're such accomplished dilettantes and no wonder so many of us die still searching for what we sought as youths. The path to realization is a wide, straight highway but, for some reason, most people prefer to wander around, lost in the forest. It's a better choice to stay focused on results rather than dabble in one thing after another without ever gaining either sustenance or substance.

Purpose is more important than achievement, and meaning trumps remuneration every time. The world around us is littered with the walking corpses of people who focus too much on conforming to an idea of what they should do and who they should be, people who worry about the opinions of others rather than about the direction set by their own inner compass. Satisfaction in our work and a sense of making a contribution to what we think is really important offer a far more reliable recipe for happiness than we can find in the accumulation of material goods or the striving for adulation and accolades.

Finding balance means emphasizing being over doing and recognizing that both lead to more happiness than having. Activities, particularly those we share with like-minded people, bring the greatest rewards. Exerting ourselves as little as possible and yet seeing everything done, the effortless act of *wu wei*, is a sign we are living the right way. When we feel depleted by our toil, it is often because we are doing the bidding of those who benefit more from our work than we do. Better to scale back to a slower, simpler life than to be a slave to someone else's agenda.

· · ·

The full weight of traditional Chinese culture rests on the shoulders of three men: Confucius, the Buddha, and Laozi, the greatest of all Daoist sages and teacher to both Zhuangzi and Confucius. Laozi was, to put it mildly, an interesting character. While there has been some debate over his historicity, recent excavations have produced multiple references confirming that he lived during the aptly named Warring States period, perhaps twenty-five hundred years ago. What I find most engaging about Laozi, beyond his obvious brilliance, is how the scant details of his life are enough to show us how he balanced the yin *of his spiritual side with the* yang *of his practical side. On the one hand, he was meditating deeply on the nature of nature and of man's role in the scheme of things. On the other, he was working as a*

librarian, a court archivist in charge of the entire body of knowledge
and wisdom of Chinese culture, although China wasn't even
China yet.

Let's look at his biography more closely. He was not only an
incandescent thinker but also a fortune teller, a royal and powerful
version of a red-light district Tarot-card-wielding flim-flam artist.
Unlike a carnival fopdoodle, of course, he used the Yijing to divine
the ways of nature and was good enough at it to be indispensable
to his boss.

Imagine this scenario: Once grand, the Zhou kingdom is steadily
shrinking. First, it has to move its capital east from the western
part of what is now China because nomadic tribes are constantly
nibbling at its borders, raiding, raping, abducting, killing, burning,
and stealing. In the newly-established eastern capital of Luoyang, the
Zhou king now faces defections by his own subjects. Lords who once
served him in an utterly obedient role have become kings in their
own right with not-insignificant lands, armies, and wealth. Instead
of serving their former master, these strongmen are willing to do no
more than pay tribute to the central government of what has become
more a loose federation than an empire. Pressured not only by these
former vassals but also by marauding nomads from both the north
and west, the king of Zhou is no happy camper.

Early one morning, the king calls Laozi to him to solicit his advice.
"Librarian," he says. "Tax revenue is thin, the army is hungry, men
are deserting, and I fear an invasion any day. I don't have enough
troops to adequately cover every border. Where will the attack come
from? Where shall I station my forces?"

Laozi retires to consider the question. To begin, he consults the Yijing
on the subject, using yarrow stalks to divine what the future holds.
Then he takes a rarely-used path down to his private meditation spot

near the river. There's a special tree there, a Chinese red oak in the midst of a field of peonies. It is still late winter so the flowers are not yet in bloom, though buds are starting to appear and the great sage smiles at the thought of the sea of color that will soon surround him in his daily ritual. Eyes closed, he stands quietly in the half-shade of the branches and watches his thoughts fly by like clouds until his mental sky clears. He wants only to return to the uncarved block that he was at birth (Daoists call this pure, undifferentiated, simple, original self P'u), before the composite chisel of his experience, history, and culture formed him into the royal fortune-teller.

When he comes back into his body, he stretches and slowly makes his way down to the river. He crouches there, ninety-eight years old but still limber enough to squat like some little girl peeling potatoes. He watches the river, timing his breath to match the circle of a leaf trapped inside an eddy. At the edges of the eddy closest to the middle of the river, the water is uncommonly clear. He leans forward slightly, the weight shifting to his toes, and peers down to the bottom. He rubs his eyes because he wants to be sure of what he sees. There is mica in the sand. The tiny mineral particles glisten and glint as they tumble and spin on their way to the sea. He smiles and takes his leave of the river, but not before he prostrates himself and offers his profuse thanks.

He spends the balance of the morning in the royal library reading marvelous scrolls from a thousand years of history and from far-off lands, each one written in one of the forty-three languages he reads and speaks and understands. In the afternoon, he visits two of his favorite concubines, plays with his great-grandchildren, drinks tea, practices with his sword and his paintbrush, and writes poetry for a short book of ideas he is putting together in preparation for his departure from the kingdom on his hundredth birthday. He sleeps well that night and awakens the next morning rested and energized. After some rice and tea, he goes to see the king.

"Sire," he says. "You must move the army to the north, and you must do it with all haste."

The king wants to be sure Laozi understand the stakes—death for them all if he's wrong, salvation for the kingdom if he's right. "You're sure?" he asks.

"I'm sure," Laozi says, producing a map from inside his robe. "We must station an ambush at this mountain pass. Our enemies will come through it any day and will not know we are expecting them. If our generals plan properly, we can inflict enough damage to geld them for a generation."

"You saw all this in a vision?" the king presses.

Laozi thinks of the message he received from the river—the mica dancing on the riverbed. Mica is not found in the loess lowlands near the capital but rather in the high moraine to the north. It has washed down only because the snows have melted early, signifying that mountain passes ordinarily blocked at this time of year are uncharacteristically open.

"I did," he says.

The king takes the great sage's counsel and sends all his men north, leaving the rest of the country defenseless. It is a stupendous gamble, but he trusts Laozi implicitly. Less than two weeks later, the Zhou army lies in wait, camouflaged cleverly, flanking the invaders and then descending upon them in a surprise attack using arrows and spears and boulders and flaming balls of oil-soaked hay. It is a total rout. The enemy is decimated and Laozi becomes the second most important man in the kingdom.

Look at the way Laozi lived. He studied. He read. He meditated. He took care of himself and achieved healthful longevity. Following the *principle of effortless action,* wu wei, *he worked only a few hours a day. Recent evidence shows he wasn't the only one. Einstein also only worked a few hours a day, spending the rest of the time honoring the needs of his mind and body by reading, resting, and thinking, thereby giving time for creative juices to flow and critical ideas to arise. We can't all be mathematical geniuses or ancient sages, but we sure can take a lesson from them. This revolutionary way of looking at life and work is actually the most natural thing in the world.*

VALUES AND CHOICES

"Weapons of mass distraction" are aimed at us without respite. Such constant stimulation is an assault on contemplation, and it is contemplation that affords us the opportunity to figure out what is important and true and to find out. In the midst of this barrage, the kind of meditative self-cultivation we need to figure out even so basic a question as who we really are and what is really important to us is lost. Such deadly daily deterrents comprise the "attention economy," a term for the aggregate of interests fighting for our eyeballs, our ears, and ultimately our dollars. This economy includes insistent media messages regarding products and services, and an entertainment complex that specializes in addictive offerings such as social media, on-demand television and movies, online pornography, and so-called "smart phones," which are addictive enough to drive constant physical compulsions. In urban areas, there are also sports bars, clubs, movie complexes, and shopping malls, all specifically designed and constructed to part us from our time and money. While some of these can be part of a balanced lifestyle, few of us can keep our use of them in check. The first step to regaining control of our lives is to tune out, turn off, take a deep breath, quiet down, and see

things through eyes unclouded by the noise others make. A
mind dominated by attention economy does not truly belong
to us and is most certainly not free.

. . .

The real purpose of material things is to serve as nodes of
interaction with each other. In the same way physics now
tells us that electrons don't exist until someone looks at
them or they are involved in some interaction, our material
romances amount to naught unless we intersect with others
around and about them. We collect widgets not so much to
gaze at them lovingly as to tell others we have them, to share
our appreciation for them, and to give us something to lust
after, acquire, and then show each other. Seen in this light, as
illuminated points in a larger fabric of communication and
society, our objects, always best kept to a minimum, become
much less interesting in and of themselves and much more
interesting in terms of who they point us to and who comes to
us as a result of our common interests.

. . .

Not so very long ago, we thought material reality was the
standard of life and living. Then physics brought us the notion
that everything is energy. More recently, quantum mechanics
has confirmed what Eastern thinkers have known for
millennia: material reality is an illusion and we are surrounded
by fields of energy. Given all these complex and nuanced
revelations about our world, we need no longer fall prey to
petty thinking that money and goods are the most important
realities. Simple living, with its emphasis on *being* rather than
having, is a sign of balanced wisdom and sophistication, not a
marker of penury, poverty, ignorance, or sloth. The simpler our

lives, the more energetically rich we are. It's time to focus on ideas, feelings, projects, and people, and thereby find freedom. It is time to become creators rather than consumers.

. . .

Many of us are more likely to paint our house than pay for a gym membership and more likely to keep our car or truck in good condition than we are to take care of our own body. Possessions often weigh us down and limit our options and our freedom. Toys and goods in moderation can give us a more interesting and comfortable life, but when we begin to think about nothing else, talk about nothing else, chase nothing else, they own us rather than the other way 'round. In the thrall of the material frenzy, we stop noticing the people in our lives, miss opportunities, and waste resources. In Daoist terms, we step out of the flow of life. When we find ourselves about to make a purchase, why not ponder if the item of our fancy will make our life easier, simpler, or more beautiful? If the answer is no, let's put our credit cards away. If we do buy something, why not give away two like items to the needy, or perhaps sell them? Instead of coveting goods, why not make a list of all the things we do *not* want? There are so very many of them out there. An expensive car (payments!), fancy china (oops, it broke), a big house (sorry I can't meet you for dinner, I have too much vacuuming to do), fancy jewelry (someone will break in and steal it or cut your hand off to get it), a big yard (all that trimming and mowing), a house on the beach (sea levels are rising, we'll wake up underwater), and on and on. Moderation is key to balancing our lives. Simplicity, even more so.

. . .

"Want," "need," and "absolutely must have" are three different things. If we talk ourselves into believing we absolutely must have something other than food, shelter, or medicine, we are victims of media manipulation regarding everything, from the kind of person we should be to the size of our waistline, our bank account, and the number of titles before our names or initials after them. The result is often to go into debt, which is exactly what those who profit from our lack of self-restraint so badly want. Debt is one of the primary tools corporate manipulators use against us. It is a form of bondage, yet it masquerades as benefit. It is a set of handcuffs and leg chains yet pretends to be a new pair of leather gloves and fancy shoes. Sometimes, loans can be incredibly helpful and important. Other times, not so much. Why not resist consumer culture and be brutally honest with ourselves about the importance of a new sports car, a big-screen television, an expensive handbag, or a washer/dryer? Why not wake up to the motivation of shylocks of questionable character, whether they operate out of a seedy pawn shop or the marble-floored halls of a corporation or bank? Freedom may be the most important thing in life; to be in debt is to lose it.

You can't keep standing on tiptoe
or walk in leaps and bounds.
You can't shine by showing off
or get ahead by pushing.
Self-satisfied people do no good,
Self-promoters never grow up.

Such stuff is to the Tao
as garbage is to food
or a tumor to the body,
hateful.
The follower of the Way
avoids it.

—Laozi Stanza 24[2]

---

2   Ursula K. LeGuin, "Lao Tzu Tao Te Ching," *A Book about the Way and the Power of the Way*, Boston and London: Shambhala, 1997

Billions of years ago, when we were simple, single-celled organisms swimming in a primordial soup, life was a moment-to-moment response to environmental changes that threatened our survival. Other than those of us living in war-torn and poverty-stricken autocracies, life need no longer be infused with this same sense of urgency and fear. Yet many of us unconsciously choose to live this way, thinking it validates our existence or proves our import. This is a false, limiting, and dangerous choice. Unless we choose to live more wisely and with greater awareness, we will continue to be propelled forward without savoring the space between the notes in the music of life. Without indulging those pauses—in which lies our most profound sense of being—the melody is lost. We all know how the story ends—we get old, we get sick, we die—so what's the hurry? The past is a memory, the future an illusion. Every moment is the only reality and each deserves our full attention. The more slowly we live, the longer we live. The longer we live, the more opportunities and experiences we have. Slowing down helps us pay attention; speeding up merely leads to a premature, unhappy demise.

• • •

Imagine your last few moments on this mortal coil. Say you step off the curb and are hit by a bus. As you lie on the street with your life seeping out, you see people point at you and scream. You watch someone dial 911 and listen to them talk desperately to the dispatcher. A few moments later, you hear the wail of an approaching ambulance but realize—in a place beyond terror and pain—that it will arrive too late. Even though I don't know you, I can pretty much guarantee you don't want your last thought to be: "That was fast, but at least I got a lot done."

Instead, of course, you hope that when your time comes you have a feeling of satisfaction, a sense that you fully engaged the people in your life, that you tried the things you wanted to try, that you felt the things you wanted to feel, that you pursued your dreams passionately, that you lived each and every moment fully and with presence. It's true that life can end at any moment—a meteor can land on your house, a fire can take you while you sleep, a stroke or heart attack can get you, you can be shot in a drive-by or bank robbery, succumb to equipment failure while scuba diving, or have the misfortune to meet the aforementioned city bus. Given all that, it's important to live fully without wasting time or effort. Living fully, however, is not the same as living quickly. In fact, I would like to argue that the best way to both live longer and get more out of life is to live at a reduced pace. It's official. My motto has become: "anything worth doing is worth doing slowly."

Apparently, I'm not the only one taken with this idea. There is a veritable explosion in activities that serve to slow down that mad rush to the end. Tai chi classes are popping up all over the country, yoga studies are doing a strong business, and, everywhere you turn, you hear someone talking about the benefits of meditation. All these healing modalities teach us to slow down and savor the unique, spectacular experience of being alive.

The moment you make that effort to gear down, you become aware of just how addicted you are to the pace of the speed-and-greed culture. You experience your own little internal yin/yang, a war that goes on inside your head between those neurons that want the constant stimulation our technology and overcrowding bring and those that crave tranquility and peace. At any given moment on any given day, one or the other side of you wins. The more often the quiet side is the victor, the more likely you are to engage that increasingly popular state of being known as mindfulness.

When you live mindfully, the quality of your life increases. Mindful, you can begin to sort through whatever health issues you have. You may discover that your hypertension, your irritable bowels, your painful joints, your migraines, your stiff back, your inability to focus, your shortness of temper, your impatience, your frustration, and even your road rage are all the consequences of your body screaming at you to slow down. Pushed and pulled along too quickly and in too many directions, you feel stressed and respond with illness; slow and mindful, you are able to prioritize what needs to be done, discard what doesn't, and enjoy the doing, too.

A slow, considered, mindful life does not mean one devoid of contribution or accomplishment—rather, it means the opposite. It is said that if you want something done, you give it to a busy person. That truism applies to reading email, mopping the floor, shipping a package, feeding the dog, or mending a broken fence. On the other hand, people who accomplish truly meaningful things are not often rushed. Deliberate, slow, mindful, and focused, they are busy in the sense of being active and focused, but they are free of frivolous demands, compulsions, and projects. Not addicted to a pace of life set by outside forces whose motivations are almost always their own profit or interests, this kind of person—the sage we all can be if we choose—concentrates his or her energy effectively on those things that really matter.

Imagine if we all lived this way. Imagine if we were willing to stop grasping at things we don't need, spending money we don't have, rushing around chasing things that don't matter, or obeying impatient bosses or even teachers who manipulate us to their own advantage by keeping the pace so frenetic we never figure things out. Taking time to notice the marvels of everyday life sounds so simple, so utopian, so hopelessly out of touch with "real" life . . . and yet, what is real? The world is as we make it, and we can make it different. Imagine the global shift we would see if everyone slowed down enough to notice what's really going on.

Body/mind practices are, at their core, all about balance. That fast, "yang" urge and that slow "yin" yearning need to be reconciled. Sometimes, after all, we need to move quickly, as in dodging the front bumper of that awful bus. What has happened to us, however, is that technology and overcrowding have driven us to live and breathe far too quickly. We don't take naps, we don't contemplate the clouds, we don't eat our food without talking or watching TV, we don't even drive our car without using our cell phones or worse, checking for messages.

The most obvious solution is to take up a body/mind practice, but that isn't the only answer. Just making the decision to slow down and be mindful can work wonders. Let's try it today. Let's just take a deep breath, stop what we're doing, look around, think about those people and things that really matter, and let go of those that don't. Then, let's slowly move on to the next experience, whether it is filling out an expense report or making love. I say it one more time: Anything worth doing is worth doing slowly.

LIFESTYLE

"Try not to try" is the perfect motto for our time, an antidote for our speed-and-greed anti-culture, and an ironic, elusive, and critically important guiding principle. Better to relax and allow things to happen than to force them out with striving and over-intellectualization. If we can only manage to get out of our own way, a seemingly magical balancing occurs. This is neither wishful thinking nor utopian delusion, but the very real and gritty nature of things.

. . .

*Given the pace of innovation at this time in human history, the news
is rife with breakthroughs. Sometimes—though never often enough—
these are revolutions in human rights, income equality, human rights,
and social policy. Now and again they are about a great artistic
achievement or the shattering of some barrier in the realm of human
mental or physical performance. Most often, however, the media is
more likely to cover technical advances with commercial potential.
Thus, we see stories about gadgets and gizmos destined to set the
market on fire, new ideas or products that will light a fire under
the design, manufacturing, marketing, and advertising sectors for
years to come.*

*In all their shiny, clever, packaged glory, such achievements may
appear to erupt as an apparent magic, yet there is always a personal
dimension to these breakthroughs. Behind each and every discovery
and advancement, there is at least one long period of sustained effort
on the part of an individual—a boatload of human sweat and toil,
representing the maturation and materialization of a vision through
the striding down a path. In short, somebody had the idea, worked
on it, massaged it, chased it, wrestled with it, and finally brought it
to fruition. Breakthroughs, then, are just points on a wave function,
a particular stage of a cycle. Behind a breakthrough, there is often
much subconscious, intuitive work. Some of this may even be in a
dream state or while meditating.*

*In the context of self-actualizing work (whether mental or physical),
breakthroughs usually follow a plateau, the often-frustrating feeling
that, for a seemingly interminable period, nothing is happening and
that there is no progress. Then, without warning, there is a sudden
flash of understanding, an aha moment or the sudden achievement
of a long sought-after goal. We try and try to quiet our mind, break a*

reflexive habit, put our palms on the floor, kick to the head, or achieve that low, quadriceps-burning posture, and then finally, we can do it.

Daoist teachings suggest that all things in the world work this way; specifically, there are periods of rest and introspection followed typically by periods of intense activity followed again by more downtime. This is true of insects at industry, of the transit of sun and moon, of squirrels going about their seasonal schedules, of the course of rivers alternately swollen with snowmelt and trickling and dry under the sun, and of human life and enterprise. Such an ongoing universal cycle is the natural manifestation of the harmonious interplay between the opposing forces of yin *and* yang *energy, between what is female, dark, quiet, mysterious, moist, and secretive, and what is male, bright, loud, evident, dry, and forthright.*

The moment of achievement is wonderful, but let's not forget the critical role of all that slogging. In trying to follow the prescriptions in this book, let's give incremental changes and improvements their due; let's appreciate the effort and time we're putting in; let's remember that every moment we spend in meditation or moving practice, every time we make a decision not to do the same old thing but to try something new, we are enacting precisely what is required to awaken and grow.

. . .

Why not choose recreational activities that enhance our enjoyment of the environment rather than destroying it? Because of the way our brain works, the faster we go, the more our vision constricts. Standing motionless on a road, sitting atop a motorcycle or within the cockpit of a race car, we may not notice the weather or the fans, but at least we see the road to be as wide as it actually is. The faster we go, the narrower that black strip before us becomes. It is no accident (pun intended) that slower activities such as surfing, sailing, climbing, diving, swimming, and hiking give us a broader view of the world and allow us to appreciate it more. Speed and risk exist in inverse proportion to wisdom and longevity. Adrenaline kills perspective just the way speed kills us, and killing ourselves often means killing the environment, too. Let's slow down and shift our emphasis. Let's engage in silent sports that strengthen us, calm our minds, use minimal resources, leave no trash behind, leave no oil film on the water and coral reefs, and keep forest paths intact. As we recreate, let's listen to the music of nature.

• • •

Drive steadily and slowly. Being behind the wheel is an opportunity to be courteous to others and do them a favor. Let others go first. Find the flow of the road and stick to it. Move effortlessly and without drawing attention to yourself in any way. Rushing about, craving the feeling of acceleration, and gaining superficial satisfaction from taking or gaining advantage on the road are all signs of a disquieted mind. The primary goal of any drive is to arrive alive. So very many people can't and don't. Is chortling about beating someone to a parking space or self-righteously forcing them off the road really the way we want to treat others and have others treat us? How much better is it to be compassionate and helpful to others on the road, to show you are aware of them as people not just drivers, as humans and not merely cars with faceless operators aboard? Next time you get behind the wheel, why not use the opportunity to relax and see if you can't find new ways to show you care for those with whom you share the road.

• • •

True relaxation has nothing to do with sitting in front of the TV with a bowl of chips and a beer. It's all about breathing mindfully and aiming our focus within. It is about body control and the release of every last bit of tension. It is about becoming as soft as overcooked fettuccine if lying down, and using just enough muscular effort to support your structure when sitting or standing. It is about understanding we have no control over the doings of the universe, that rather than forcing things to happen, we should just let them unfold and appreciate their magic. Once the mind and body are free of tension, we are free to see things as they really are, to avoid wasting time and energy, and to be a maximally effective participant in life.

...

Smartphone and computer addictions mean we're having less sex. Seriously? Yes. Why would we rather stare at a little glowing screen than touch each other? Scientific investigation suggests that the smart phone is the crack cocaine of technology, offering an irresistible combination of visual and tactile attraction and feedback. Here's a good tip for a better sex life: *Keep laptops, tablets, and phones out of the bedroom.* Install a music system instead. Rocking and rolling means more than just hitting drums and fingering frets. Enjoy sex and music together and let the only glow come from a candle or, even better, from each other.

...

Contemporary hookup culture flies against the advice of Daoist thought in a couple of ways. First and foremost is the compassionate dimension. In the same way that indifference— not hate—is the opposite of love, casual sex, especially sex performed under the influence of alcohol or other drugs, is the pinnacle of disconnection from another person. It is a violation of trust and intimacy. While Daoism touts sex as an important energetic route to enhanced health and character, it is far less effective when it does not involve a deep emotional connection. In addition to the risk of communicable disease, such activities inevitably leave psychological scars, particularly on female, minority, or LBGTQ participants.

...

The art of conversation used to be seen as one of life's great pleasures and treasures, the meat-and-potatoes of human interaction. These days, conversation has relinquished ground to email notes and texted messages. This is a great loss, for face-to-face interaction is the source of compassion and altruism, the very glue that holds human society together. The first and most important thing a conversation does is to allow, encourage, or force us to acknowledge the presence of another human being. This is not a small thing, for there is no greater gift we can give another person than to recognize he or she exists and has a point of view, and no more healing thing than to validate their experience, especially their pain. As a consequence of presenting issues, ideas, and events in a fashion different from our own (but often no less legitimate or correct), conversation also encourages or requires us to grow. In the case of conversation, as the old saw goes, the medium really *is* the message.

...

Penmanship is a lost art. Perhaps it is time we set aside our trackpads, mice, keyboards, and styli, and find pleasure instead in a soft nib of just the right width and a good pen barrel that fits our palm and fingers. Time to explore the word of inks in

bottles or cartridges and use both color and the appearance
of letters as a way to express ourselves slowly, carefully,
deliberately, and in an old way that may be new to us. Fountain
pens and fine paper have never been more varied or beautiful,
inks never more colorful, and the opportunities to learn fine
handwriting, calligraphy, or Chinese characters never greater.
On this subject, even pencils merit reconsideration. There are
some beautifully made ones that write like a dream, their tips
gliding effortless across paper. Whatever the instrument, there
is something about a handwritten love note, thank-you note,
or heartfelt letter that completely eclipses the mundane piece
of email or banal text message. Abiding quietly, focused on the
sound of our own writing and on the formation of beautiful
circles and lines, we slow our breathing, shrink the world, relax
our mind, and combat stress.

· · ·

Traveling has its pleasures for those who can afford it. It can
also be a fount of inspiration for artists and architects of
public policy. Yet Laozi, the great Daoist sage, reminds us that
everything necessary for a balanced and fulfilling life can be
found close to home. The most transcendent journey takes
place within us. The most profound wisdom is offered by
nature. The greatest pleasure comes from sharing time, energy,
and positive ideas with those near and dear to us. None of
these things require journeying to exotic destinations.

· · ·

Ignorance is not an excuse for destructive, selfish behavior.
Finding the impetus and discipline to learn is one of the key
elements of a life lived well. Learning can happen through life
experiences or through structured coursework. Best of all,

it can happen effortlessly, sometimes by accident, and often unconsciously in hobbies, pastimes, and passions. When the engine of an inquiring mind is fed the fuel of either necessity or desire, it thrums and races in the most balanced and beautiful way.

. . .

A simple consciousness-raising exercise is to notice how many times we discard charitable appeals in the form of mail coming to us from advocacy groups, often with images of children or animals on the envelope. Rather than shopping or dining out, we could open them and become familiar with what people are doing for each other, for the environment, and for other sentient beings. Times may be lean for many of us, but they are not so lean that we can't extend a hand to those in need. Even if we are on a crushing budget, we could send a dollar or two to the ones we find most compelling. If we're doing well financially, we might wish to make a donation that really changes the fate of the hungry children, the silent trees, the slaughtered creatures, the gasping, polluted oceans. Get this: The long and persuasive tentacles of nefarious corporations notwithstanding, we are *not* first and foremost consumers. Rather, we are conscious beings with responsibilities to each other and to the Earth. Simply deciding to care is an act that resonates in the world by rebalancing unfairness and inequity.

. . .

Right living means supporting others and contributing to the greater good whilst pursuing our own goals. It means being efficient, which is to say, achieving maximum results with minimum effort. It means quieting the mind and body until the pulsing buzz of life on Earth is clearly audible. It means abandoning fixed plans in favor of a willingness to go wherever the river of life takes us. Embracing compassion, frugality, humility, service, creativity, non-conformity, and freedom helps us stay out of our own way. Following these values and ideals, we are more likely to be able to find satisfaction, hope, love, and joy.

Tao doesn't do anything,
And yet somehow it gets everything done.
If the mighty could also eschew objectives,
Everything in the world would naturally thrive.

When objectives assert themselves,
They can be subdued with simplicity.
Subdued by simplicity, tranquility is attained,
And the world once again thrives as it may.

—Laozi Stanza 37[3]

---

3   Oliver Benjamin, *The Tao Te Ching*, Abide University Press, 2016.

Conservation and preservation (subtly different ideas) are lifestyle and philosophical choices, not the idle indulgences of granola-eating liberals. Both terms can apply to either natural resources or man-made wonders such as great works of art or architecture. To focus on the distinction between conservation and preservation is to lose the larger point, which is an appreciation of beauty, a sense of wonder, and a recognition of what is significant in the world. Both conservation and preservation flow naturally from compassion, because living beings are often affected by our choices. Conservation and preservation involve frugality, too, because they remind us that we must always be conscious that our world's resources are limited and finite. Conservation and preservation cultivate humility, as well, because gratitude and respect for others and for our home planet are the bedrocks of sagely living and successful human society. Accordingly, why not incorporate conservation and preservation into our every act and gesture, thought, and choice?

...

There are so very many small choices we can make which, when added together, signal a sea change in our values. If we all did them, of course, we would have a significant impact on the world. An example is buying fairly traded goods. Are such products perfect? Of course not. There are always scams and there are always unsubstantiated claims and practices. Yet workers benefit from fair trade and the act of bringing consciousness to the marketplace is a step in the direction of the redistribution of global wealth. Simply sending the signal you care about the people who pick tea leaves, harvest coffee beans, and sweat in factories to make running shoes, clothes, and personal electronic devices is an important and valuable action in our consumer world. Buyer action commands seller attention.

...

"You're such a complicated person."

"This is a complex deal."

"It's complicated. You wouldn't understand."

In our speed-and-greed anti-culture, the words "complex" and "complicated" have reached a kind of cult status. To be complicated means to have depth, smarts, education, your fingers in a lot of pies, many people in your life, hot prospects, and more than a few pots on burners. The people our media adulates—and thus the folks many of us look up to—are those with complex deals in the offing, complex living arrangements, complicated travel schedules, complicated contracts and options, and complex choices to make. They are our celebrity entertainers, our politicians, our queens of fashion and captains of industry.

A complicated relationship is, despite the suggestion of unrequited love and underlying angst, the kind most of us have with our loved ones or those we would love. A complex career is the one we want, as it is more likely to provide future opportunity and multiple income sources, and more likely to make us feel, or be, indispensable and irreplaceable. A complicated mind is one that produces ideas on many fronts, one that is able to spew out, if not take in, various data in an efficient and organized way. As science reveals our universe to be far more complex than we thought, complicated new theories have arisen (string theory, in the new physics, for example) to explain how things work. Complexity, it seems, is the rage of the day.

And yet there is no spiritual tradition that advocates a complicated life. People who have calmed and quieted their mind with meditation and body/mind practice know that it is simplicity, not complexity, that leads to deep thinking, pure awareness, and clear perception. Such practitioners know that the complicated behavior we call multitasking is just doing many things poorly at the same time. They know, too, that an overly complicated life, one that keeps a person endlessly busy, always plugged-in, available, and aimed at ticking off one more entry on their to-do list, can also be a life full of addiction, avoidance, and disquiet.

Certainly, we can say that the pace of modern life, increased and supported by our technology in general and our personal electronics in particular, has resulted in a short attention span and an addiction to the influx of information. A mind so conditioned has little opportunity to think critically and even less chance to experience life deeply by being in the present moment. A complex life with complicated activities, relationships, and commitments implies a reflexive busy-ness that supplants true thinking and feeling with knee-jerk reactions. It is a life high in stress and light on substance, at least in the spiritually meaningful dimensions of being.

Are you aware that your life has become too complicated? Are you always rushing to catch up? Do you find yourself doing so many things at once that you barely remember the day, cannot recall what you've accomplished, don't remember thinking hard, or feeling anything especially keenly? Do you feel you are stressed by all the "shoulds" of your life, by the countless material things you must keep track of and care for, by the endless commitments you've made, the formidable list of titillations you find yourself unable to ignore, the responsibilities you have shouldered in order to feel more substantial, more a contributing member of society, more an important personage? If so, it may well be time to simplify your life.

Start with the easy part. Attack your garage, your closet, those kitchen drawers in which you dump everything. The number of things you call yours is likely the number of steps you are away from enlightenment, and a materially cluttered life just gives you more excuses not to think about life's important issues. Stop puttering around with your stuff. Throw things away, give them away, sell them. Thin out. Cut down.

Next, work on your ability to say no to invitations, suggestions, more commitments. Look hard at the reasons you're afraid not to go to dinners and parties even when you're tired or in the mood to stay home. Ask yourself why you think you have to be everywhere all the time, what you worry others might think of you, why you care so much. Remember, time spent simply and quietly, no matter what your age or station in life, can benefit you by giving you the peace and quiet you need to bring your body and mind into harmony. Organize your schedule in the direction of less wasted time and effort and less running around.

Simplicity is purity. It is facing the true nature of things and embracing it, instead of ducking and weaving and dodging, instead of filling a hole inside you with chaotic activity or an overabundance of stuff. A simple wardrobe, a simple routine, a simple home, a simple lifestyle, simple, straightforward, meaningful relationships—these words describe freedom not limitation, intensity not distraction, focus not mental fog, a life fully lived not a life of lack. A simple life is a deep life.

Years ago, trend-watchers began to say that less is more. Today, it's clear that simple is simply better.

• • •

Our culture finds complexity beguiling. Not only do we have academic disciplines around modeling it mathematically, we often mistake it for depth in a person. Complicated people are seen as smarter, deeper, more aware of things in the world, and more attractive during mating rituals and in the hiring process. This is ironic, because complexity is often at odds with self-awareness and self-discipline and may even lead to an exaggerated sense of self that introduces opacity rather than transparency to our thinking. If there is a single key to the lock on spiritual growth, achievement, awareness, and awakening, that key is simplicity.

CHAPTER THREE

FOSTERING
COMMUNITY,
DEEPENING CULTURE

O nce we have prepared the body and opened the mind, the natural next step is to look about and see what we can do with our newfound insight and understanding. One of the first things we come to realize is that, in spite all of the work we have done on ourselves, we cannot and must not "go it alone." Indeed, it is the non-dual nature of Daoism that awakens us to see ourselves as connected to each other and the natural world around us. This runs totally counter to the myth of human superiority, the religious notion of hegemony over the planet, and the narcissistic, macho individualism of modern Western culture.

Going it alone, the cult of the self-reliant individual, likely stemmed from the challenges settlers faced in making a home for themselves in North America, a land populated by people who had adapted to life here over the course of millennia. In the time since then, self-reliance (of the frontier sort, not Ralph Waldo Emerson's recommended distance from deities and organized religion) has become one of our culture's most pervasive and pernicious myths. In truth, nobody survives long term on their own—not now, not then, not ever. Even hunter-gatherers gathered, and not just in the sense of picking edible roots. Survival on the frontier was tough and entailed hardening to the suffering of the land and its native people. It also required people to work together and help each other. Sadly, greed, ignorance, and tribalism ruled, and our ancestors banded together successfully to not only survive but commit genocide against the indigenous populations. This horror is rendered quite differently, and grossly inaccurately, by films in the "Western" genre.

If karma exists—it is not a Daoist concept—then surely the violence we experience today is a function of our genocidal roots. As we did to others, so we can expect to have done to us. We must face our history square on, not sugarcoat it the way we do our religious myths. So faced, it becomes clear that a healthy village is better than a frontier homestead standing alone against the wind. A healthy village is one where people cooperate, share a vision for the world, and live free from tyranny exercised by them or upon them. What we hope for in our personal circle is to find like-minded people and work with them for the benefit of all sentient beings.

This work spreads out like a spiritual ripple whose center is us. It begins with our family. It continues into our community of neighbors, friends, and coworkers. It is about what behaviors are and are not acceptable. It is about the annihilation of prejudice and presumption, and about escaping the shackles of clubbishness and vagaries of commercial pop culture which exist to enslave us financially, to reduce us intellectually, and to numb us to the real world using various forms of entertainment. It is about which values and priorities and norms we should accept and which we should reject, all the while remembering that, in the same way we distinguish between the mind virus of religious superstition and those it infects, we must separate the mind virus of a culture that seeks to control and diminish us from those who must live inside it. It is about a resetting of the context and content of our relationships with others, and, ultimately, the rest of the living world. It is about recognizing the forward flow of time and how it changes our perceptions of both the exotic and the familiar, lending new meaning and context to shared experience, and to objects and subjects about which we may have strong opinions and beliefs. It is about Dao, which, please remember, is a process, not an entity.

CARING AND LEARNING

I recently read a newspaper story about a Florida man who so neglected his ninety-year-old mother that her shoes "grew into her feet." The story alleged that the son lived with the elderly woman but took no care of her hypertension or diabetes. Aware of her need for twenty-four-hour medical care, he chose not to provide it. In addition to starving her, he left her atop a feces-ridden carpet. He claimed to not have a good relationship with her. Charges were filed against him and he was arrested. This story has been followed by horrifying revelations of nursing home abuse, financial scams against the elderly, and an increase in the population of elderly homeless. At the same time, perhaps ironically, end-of-life care is generally improving and people are living longer, though not so much longer in this country as in countries with superior healthcare systems.

At a time when our country is polarized between left and right, liberal and conservative, interior and coast, fundamentalists and secularists, black and white, it is troubling to find a burgeoning divide between young and old. It seems young, self-satisfied, tech-savvy people increasingly harbor for previous generations of people the same disdain they harbor for old technology. Elderly people don't go bad like milk or yoghurt. They don't have a date after which they are no good. To treat them as if they do, to shut them away in homes and leave them to die unappreciated, lonely, disconnected, and superfluous, is to make a cruel and cosmic blunder.

The elderly can teach us things about living. They may not have great reflexes behind the wheel but their brains have developed effective nonsense meters: the ability to separate the useful time-wasters of life from the meaningful projects. Benefiting from experience and perspective that the rest of us lack, and being excruciatingly aware of their mortality, older people are less likely to commit the gravest social mistakes. They don't, for instance, accumulate things they don't need, bought with money they don't have. They are more likely to pursue connections with others, act compassionately, and refrain from the type of judgments than they are to pursue wealth or fame.

Disdaining the elderly is part of a larger trend of discarding so much of what came before. This is foolish. Why consign ourselves to repeat the mistakes of previous generations? Is doing so not a guarantor of trials and tribulations? Could it be that trashing the past is the root of our dissatisfaction with the most opulent, luxurious, and technologically advanced lifestyle in the history of mankind? Deep down, we cannot feel calm and clear when we have cut the cord from what came before us and set ourselves adrift. Reevaluating what the elderly have to offer may stabilize our spinning moral compass. Literally and figuratively embracing our elderly relatives and friends may be a fine way out of the ache of moral meaninglessness.

Traditional Chinese culture is far older than our own and has had more time to mature and set wise priorities. It is the traditional Chinese way to share our homes with our grandparents and even our great-grandparents. To this day, many religious Daoists define themselves according to lineage and ancestry. We don't have to go this far. We can start with smaller steps like performing acts of service for elderly neighbors. Why not mow a lawn, carry groceries, pick up trash, make a run to the drugstore, open a jar, fix a leak, walk a pet, clean up a room, play a game of cards, or just stop by for a cup of tea? Moreover, we can keep the elderly in mind when we design cities, which is where most elderly people reside. We can make parks and pools and buildings friendlier to those with limited physical abilities, and easier to access and utilize, too. Let's bring senior citizens back into the mainstream of our culture as the valued, appreciated, and important people they should be. Let's please remember that our elders are us in a few years. We are all getting older, right from the start, right from day one.

We are all the same.

· · ·

While most households in the world are richly multigenerational, it is not in vogue for most of us to share our homes with older and younger family members. The kind of impatient self-absorption (it's all about us and gratifying our desire for freedom, luxury, and convenience) that leads us to want to live by ourselves runs deeply counter to both filial piety and basic compassion. Until and unless they are in need of constant medical attention, shunting the elderly to homes and care facilities is a callous practice. Have we simply forgotten the most basic truths about the trajectory of human life? How can we possibly discriminate against the very people we will eventually become, against those who have lived longer than we have, learned more, shared more, and done more? Let's keep our children around for as long as we can and legislate for programs and assistance for at-home care for the elderly. Let's welcome our parents into our own homes and show them the respect they deserve. Let's make it our business not to categorize and stereotype older people but to treasure and learn from them as the resources of experience and founts of wisdom they are. Let's work hard to eliminate age-based workplace discrimination, and to alleviate the loneliness and pain that often comes with age. Let's stamp out institutional elder abuse wherever it rears its ugly head.

. . .

A parent is not a sperm or an egg donor; a parent is someone
who parents. Parenting may be the most critical role we play in
our lives. Not only must we put our children before ourselves,
we must reach out into the world to help the needy. There are
so very many children in need of adoption or foster care. Why
not share what you know, what you feel, what you love, and
what you have with a child who desperately needs your care
and who will carry your legacy out into the world?

. . .

Merely two generations ago, teens in our country protested
against war, traveled abroad with backpacks, and worked
in the Peace Corps. Today, many are about as competent as
a kangaroo's clinging joey, unable to find their way to the
end of the street without computer assistance. Many don't
know how to say "thank you" to their parents nor "please"
to strangers, don't understand their place in the world, don't
make their beds, clean the kitchen, do the dishes, walk the dog,
or appreciate how fortunate they are to be fed and clothed and
housed and schooled when those basics escape so many. If our
children take the love and lives we give them for granted, we
have no one to blame but ourselves. We may wish we could
care-take our children forever, but soon they will have to make
their way in a world that promises them absolutely nothing
at all. Is it not time to disabuse them of any notion of material
entitlement, to develop their discipline, to instill in them a
respect for natural resources and the rights of all sentient
beings, and cultivate in them compassion, frugality, and
humility? We must teach them the benefits of a simple, natural
life, the primacy of concepts over facts, and pattern recognition
over rote memory. We must encourage their love of learning by

emphasizing personal expression over test performance, self-cultivation over obedience, and independence over conformity. We have no more important task than to share such powerful and formative ideas with our children and to help them to implement those ideas in their everyday life.

. . .

The noise and overstimulation of videogames have taken our children hostage. Some such games may sharpen our hand-to-eye reflexes, but they generally foreshorten our attention spans, dull our emotions and creativity, and may even deprive us of empathy. Digital technology is certainly the new frontier, yet, without the ability to concentrate on the kind of complex arguments found in books we become easy targets for predatory corporations and totalitarian regimes. Allowing children to become mortally addicted—yes, the addiction can be fatal—to glowing screens is to guarantee they remain sheep while the wolves run the world. We may not be able to reverse the trend but we can balance and counter it with trips to deserts and forests, and with poetry, which begins where science ends and invites us to experience everything more deeply. Let's show our children the glory of nature, teach them to move and to build things with their hands, then stand back and watch as they change the world. We have nothing more important to do.

. . .

Every time we tune in, download, or line up to watch violent entertainment with negative messages, we encourage the entertainment conglomerates to give us more of the same. Every time we elect a candidate who flip-flops on issues and talks out of both sides of his mouth, we rig the system to bring us another like him. Why not choose lovers, not fighters, as our screen heroes? Why not support programming, games, and films that promote the preservation of nature rather than the shedding of blood? At very least, let's try some European sword-and-sorcery tales and treat ourselves to Chinese *wuxia* films, Japanese samurai flicks, and modern Korean martial masterpieces, all of which elevate crude violence to visual art, thereby disconnecting it from the real world. Better yet, watch documentaries about nature. They contain all the violence any sane person could ever crave while, at the same time, offering an opportunity for reverence and wonder.

. . .

The gladiatorial impulse seems to run strongly through the naked ape as well as others. In sporting contests ranging from cage fighting to team sports, we beat flex our muscles, show our speed, jump and leap and contend with bare hands, feet, sticks, rackets, and clubs. Perhaps this impulse is linked to sex hormones, as both men and women like to compete among themselves, and both men and women like to watch the opposite sex do so. Perhaps it derives from the sad and outdated notion that nature is all about catching prey, hiding from predators, hoarding food, and protecting our den or tree or hole. Whatever the root, competitive behavior is anachronistic if not downright atavistic. The immediate cost is to the health and lives of the participants in games like football, mixed martial arts, and boxing. The larger cost occurs in the audience of events broadcast to millions, who come to see physical conflict as a desirable method of settling differences and suffer from an overall violent cultural tone. Let's ban such sports in favor of those that still allow us to celebrate physical prowess but don't lead to dire injuries of body, psyche, and society.

• • •

Celebrity worship—most commonly of uneducated antiheroes, entertainers, and self-aggrandizing politicians—is an insidious disease of modern Western culture. Most celebrities live in sharp opposition to the principles of humility, compassion, and frugality. The choices, values, and lifestyles that contribute to the formation of the enlightened person often lead such a person to go unnoticed in today's speed-and-greed world. When we do encounter a sage, she seems to live a life of effortless invisibility, supporting others in their efforts rather than personally seeking attention. It does not speak well of us that we pay more attention to superficialities than to deeper acts and to those who cry "look at me" rather than to those who actually do meaningful and important work. If there is no way to avoid adulating celebrities, then why not shift our standards of measure to appreciate caregivers, parents, educators, researchers, and those who put their lives on the line for others? While we're at it, what say we stop taking pictures of ourselves, too? "Selfie" culture is no culture at all.

• • •

If Mark Twain had been deprived of the opportunity to wander down a country lane with a piece of grass sticking out of his mouth, would he have been able to create the characters he did? No quiet time in the country, I say, no Tom Sawyer and Huck Finn. Would today's Twain instead spend his time in linked Internet videogame shooting championships and then put it all aside at night to pen a world where superhero assassins work for secret government factions, have intimate relations with enemy spies, then go on to save the world? Frankly, I don't think he could have summoned the necessary concentration. The primacy given to newsbytes and online short content has shortened our attention spans and reduced our mental ability to perform sustained tasks. The result? Not only the slow death of the book but a retreat from contemplation, profound thinking, journaling and long-form work of all kinds.

As we speed up, I can't help but think we are buzzing like bees around a damaged hive. A fast life is a cheap life and a cheap life is devoid of deep experience, including the appreciation of art. Such penury reduces the meaning of everything. The point of a novel is not merely to savor a finely crafted plot and believable characters who touch our hearts, but to learn more about reality by seeing the world, painstakingly rendered (I speak here more of serious writing than pulp or genre fiction) through the eyes of another. If we are not able to sustain our concentration sufficiently to do this, we are missing so very, very many of nature's cues and clues, including the messages we send each other through a tremble in the voice or a twitch of the face. Absent this information, we are looking no deeper than the surface of the pond of life, living exactly the way I wanted so badly not to live when I was a child.

Time is being whipped into a frenzy by the deluge of information. A study by the famous philosopher/psychologist Robert Ornstein established that the human brain marks the passage of time on the basis of how much information it receives. A commuter who sees the same scenery rush by the train window every morning, for example, finds the ride to work of far lesser duration than his seatmate who has never taken the ride before. This is because the new rider is fascinated by what he sees looking out the window and processes more data—the houses, the cars, the people, the river, the rhythm of the wheels, the smell of the vinyl, the click clack of the conductor's ticket punch— than the habitual rider. More data means more external reality, and it is to external reality that we look to mark the passage of time.

There's another clock, of course, and that is the one inside us. Myriad ongoing biological processes have rates of their own, from the life and death of the red corpuscle to the muscular contractions of our atria and ventricles. If we were perfectly centered beings floating on carpets of enlightened thread, communing with pelicans and showering in rain clouds, these processes would be at a low, throbbing, pulsing, healthy level. Unfortunately, what goes on around us has an intimate and immediate effect on our biological clock, our respiratory rate, our heart rate, our metabolism, and on the firing of our nerves and the release of our hormones.

As I write this, researchers have won the Nobel Prize for their work in figuring out the molecular clock ticking in all living things. Their work took place in fruit flies and has implications on what controls our mood, our health, our behavior, our memory, our mental function, and more. In order to honor that clock, we must pay attention to the messages we receive from our body. We can't hear those messages when we are engrossed in tiny glowing screens or subjecting ourselves to larger versions of the same, replete with explosions and their thunderous noise and bright flashes.

Instead, let's slow down, quiet down, and engage the thoughts and feelings of others, particularly those we find in books, which have been put forward with industry and care. In doing so, we will heal much of the damage done to our brains by digital technology. To extend our repair of what has become broken, rather than downloading the book onto an electronic reader (it's not really a book if we can't hold it in your hand), let's buy real books from independent brick-and-mortar bookstores, places where we can have the pleasure of meeting other readers—often smart sales staff eager to recommend favorite titles—while indulging the tactile experience of feeling the cover in our hands and turning crisp, white pages to find worlds of wonder within. Reading is a meditation all its own.

. . .

Because high technology can and does provide important solutions and tools for modern living, creative achievements in the field—particularly in engineering and design—receive more commercial and media attention than similar efforts in other fields. Even so, the beauty inherent in the work of comparatively low-tech artisan may do more to stir the spirit. Technology can excite, but hand-crafting satisfies. It is high time for a renewed celebration of individual artistry and craftsmanship, the best of which represents insight into urges and feelings we all share and skills we all admire.

. . .

When fine arts are the province of only the privileged and rich, a great source for joy and spiritual transcendence is withheld from the eager majority who need it most. The phrase "art for art's sake" underestimates art's importance. Art awakens us to the designs and forces at work in our world. It is a gateway to *Dao*. Let's work to see free museum admission, increased focus on the arts in education, and expanded governmental patronage of public venues for exhibits.

. . .

The human brain is wired for story. This may be a direct result of the pressures of natural selection upon the evolution of our brain or it may be a result of our mind's trajectory through language and culture. Perhaps both processes are inextricable. Literature of all kinds helps us interpret the world. It deepens our understanding of who and what we really are. In aboriginal cultures, storytelling high priests and shamans were responsible for the population's world view. Their most satisfying and worthwhile tales were those that moved their audience toward conscious awakening. As it was in the past, so it is today. Stories still have immense power, so we must voluntarily choose those that inspire, motivate, and uplift us spiritually. Let's find them in literary novels, comic books, pulp fiction, and classical mythology. In turn, let's ignore those pundits—rampant in mainstream media—whose stories contain hidden commercial agendas, instill fear, and encourage conformity.

...

Music is a language that transcends all borders. Its messages and memes penetrate popular culture faster than those found in any other medium. Unfortunately, this highly potent vehicle for the transmission of feelings and ideas has fallen under the control of a few manipulative corporate entities. This sorry state of affairs disrupts the quintessential bond between artist and audience. The result is that, although there is more and more varied music accessible to all for free, the music we listen to through earbuds and headphones has been compressed to the point of painful sanitation. Worse, musicians are underpaid and starving. Let's break monopolies and support musicians by purchasing or accessing music from sources allying themselves with artists first and industry second. Musician websites are best. Support performers directly whenever possible. Encourage artistic freedom, self-expression, and the survival of authentic souls by paying for what you enjoy. Try listening to music live or through proper music systems that actually move air. Savor the sound of vacuum tube electronics and vinyl sources.

THINKING AND THRIVING

When a western field biologist sees a new and unknown frog in a pond, he grabs it and unceremoniously drops it into a bottle of formaldehyde, a preservative that doubles as a deadly poison. Frogs respire through their skin, so the "specimen" dies a burning, suffocating, agonizing death. Next, the biologist removes the corpse from the bottle, pins the little guy's legs out wide on a tray of hard wax, and cuts into it with a scalpel to have a look at what's inside. He is seeking to link the frog to other frogs known to science, hoping for a sense of where this new creature fits into the phylogenetic tree.

He might pay some passing attention to the frog's stomach contents, maybe note them in a file on his computer ("eats crickets"), before pulling out other organs to assess their level of development and their morphology. He examines the heart and lungs to learn about its circulatory system, and the reproductive tract, too. If he's lucky, the little guy might turn out to be a little girl and he might find some gelatinous eggs that will now never be laid, thereby diminishing the overall frog population even at a time when amphibians are among the rarest and most endangered creatures on planet Earth. After that, he might examine the frog under a microscope, perhaps even an electron microscope, drawing a bead on the structure of the frog's eyes, its brain, and more. Last but not least, he will take a DNA sample (okay, he would have done this before he dropped the frog into formaldehyde) and then, if possible, he might even be able to clone the dead frog and watch it hop around.

At this point, he has a pretty good picture of the frog's cladistics, but I would argue he is missing much essential information about "frog-ness." Put another way, he has a decent idea of who the frog's closest relatives are but is no closer to understanding what it is to be a frog. To fathom that, he has to see a frog alive in its environment, watch how its eyes respond to movement, and how it chases and eats its prey. He needs to know how it swims when floodwaters come, how it digs a hole to find mud when there's a drought, how it finds a mate in spring, how it carries its babies on its back (or holds them in its mouth for safety), and how a tadpole becomes an adult frog. Watching this last amazing transformation, he can even see a recapitulation of a frog's evolution, beginning as a creature close to a fish, and morphing to a different creature altogether.

Understanding a frog's quintessence requires either meditative enlightenment or, more accessibly, system-think. Science in general, and biology in particular, is increasingly moving in the direction of putting things together to understand them instead of taking them apart. That's where we get ecology, population biology, and a plethora of emerging disciplines that represent the coalescence of previously distinct ones. Our long Western history of deconstruction is giving way to synthesizing the way Eastern philosophy does. First we made everything separate, then we looked at the way things interrelate, then we went to the quantum level and found that everything really is one. In other words, we've taken what was simple, made it very complicated, and found ourselves looking for the simple again in order to achieve deeper understanding.

Incidentally, we've done the same things to music that we've done to frogs. We've taken the sounds made by real people in real life on real instruments and recorded them. Then we've compressed that information to make it easier to store and copy and retrieve. The result? Music today is to live, real music as an origami frog is to a real one. Music has, in short, been dumbed down.

One consequence of so many thin recordings lacking in detail is that those of us who have rarely, if ever, heard live (especially acoustic) music actually prefer it to better quality sound. In fact, some studies show that young people who listen to music on personal devices don't care much for the real thing, the *yin* and *yang* of highs and lows and the atmosphere of harmonics and all. A number of famous musicians have complained about this and released their music on higher quality discs. Aware that something has been lost, some music lovers are starting to look for it again. Audiophiles, now a beleaguered, endangered minority of listeners, are fighting back. Digital recordings are now being enhanced to sound more like analog, and transistor electronics are now being melded with (and sometimes replaced by) old-style vacuum tubes in an effort to restore live music's warmth and ambience.

There is a trend here, and it runs from biology to musicology. The trend is to diminish the richness of information, to deprive the human sensorium and the human intellect both, to speed up and thin out experiences ranging from the marvel of a living creature to the beauty of music. Substitutes of the true nature of things with a convenient, cheapened simulacrum goes against Dao.

Let's do ourselves a favor and spend more time in the natural world, simply savoring it rather than analyzing it. Let's enjoy real music, too, rather than a watered-down version. Let's hear a live performance, preferably in a small and intimate setting with acoustic instruments played at a moderate level. Even better, let's find a live orchestra performing classical greats. Why not taste the violin's strings on our tongue the way the frog feels the footsteps of a passing cricket? Why not feel the tremble of the jazz singer's voice, the twang of a folk musician's banjo, the boom of the bass? Why not discover how much

emotion, how much pleasure, and how much pure sensation
there is to be had when the full range of music hits our ears?
The experience of live music remains one of life's finest and
most therapeutic pleasures. It's good for what ails us!

· · ·

Why not enlist technology in service to our highest ideals
rather than employ it in pursuit of our transient and
unquenchable appetites? Working ethically within the
constraints of resources is the mark of real creative genius.
Can we not manufacture things that last rather than support
an economy founded upon planned obsolescence, greed, and
instant gratification? When planned, obsolescence becomes
a crime and throwing things away becomes anathema. If a
product requires any advertising other than an announcement
of its function and availability, it is probably of more value to
the seller than the buyer and thus not much worthwhile.

· · ·

Science and its unruly offspring, technology, are useful and
important tools appropriate for many practical and important
jobs in our complex, modern world. They can, however, lead
us to hubris. Let's stay humble in the face of the unknowable
universe. We can never really be sure of anything. Anytime
we feel intellectual certainty about anything, let's remember
that we stand, at every moment, on cosmic quicksand. In
fact, nature is so complex that our brain's primary job is to
act as a filter protecting us from the unimaginable torrent
of information constantly coming our way. Light must be
constrained into just a tiny portion of available wavelengths
lest we are blinded by all there is to see. Sound must be
moderated lest too many frequencies prevent us from

hearing melodies, spoken words, or alarms that spell danger. Chemosensation must be limited to either what is immediately toxic (so we can avoid it) or those pheromones that guide our reproductive and social interaction; lest we lose ourselves in the titillations of taste, our brain allows us only to recognize passion and poison. The takeaway? Eschew dogmatism and beware any statement beginning with "the fact is."

· · ·

To understand the world, scientists are wont to take things apart into their component parts, rather than assembling them into systems. True and complete understanding comes from employing both approaches. We can take things apart so long as we cause no suffering and do no harm, but we need to put them back into the context of the larger universe to truly appreciate larger truths and the marvels of nature.

· · ·

The modern Western brain is trained to learn in bits and bytes. Conditioned by hyperlinks, which are addictively fast, effortless, we are learning to follow the path of least resistance in the flow of information. This sounds good on the surface—Daoism is all about going with the flow—but this flow is artificial, not natural. It is human nature to contemplate and cogitate rather than skim data like a butterfly over a pond. Hyperlinking exposes us to much new information and *can* serve deep thinking if one uses it for that purpose. Unfortunately, for most folks, it interrupts concentration on a single point or idea rather than sustains it, and discourages the application of our critical rational faculties, too. Because online learning is generally more passive than active, discrimination (asking if a presented fact is really true and if a source is reliable) has become one of its casualties. We are, in short, being trained to substitute shallow experience for deep thinking, and short-term titillation for the long-term satisfaction of sustained focus. This stands in sharp contrast to the way Daoist wisdom is passed down, which is through example, shared experience, and conversations between people of different generations. Computers can't teach wisdom. It is not available on the Internet in anything other than ersatz form. It is in full flower, however, in the elderly.

...

Accepting what we are told as true is okay when we're children, but growing up means opening our eyes, gazing unflinchingly at offensive things, and thinking critically about the messages society and multimedia present. When we do this, we find that some of what we have learned is accurate and unbiased, while much of it expresses—with varying degrees of subtlety—the aims and agendas of those in our community who seek to control, exploit, or sell us something. Spending time online and with broadcast media, why not choose your information sources with circumspection? Why not question and verify what does not seem right or true?

...

One of the first martial arts I studied was Kenpo Karate. Despite the Japanese-sounding name, this is a contemporary Western style that blends traditional Chinese, Japanese, and sometimes, Korean and Indonesian arts. Kenpo was made famous by a Hawaii-born practitioner and then brought to Hollywood, where it was favored by action stars. Kenpo remains a practical style taught to devotees around the world by many organizations. After being awarded a black belt in this system, I opened a franchised school under the umbrella of one such outfit.

One day, I was summoned by the system's grandmaster and went for an audience with him at his flagship school. My own school was still a fledgling business and I thought perhaps that he was going to castigate me for not bringing in more students and more money. I found the grandmaster behind an expansive desk in a room densely decorated with Asian paintings and sculptures. He was flanked by four large men, all of whom enjoyed legendary reputations for aggression and skill. They stared at me intently, arms crossed.

"I hear you're a very good fighter," the grandmaster began without preamble.

"Actually, I'm more interested in seeing my students get healthy, gain confidence, and use the philosophical ideas in their daily lives. I'm trying to build a community around the school."

The four henchmen chuckled derisively. The grandmaster raised his eyebrows, then unceremoniously produced a large attaché case from underneath his desk. I recognized it as a famous brand, constructed from aluminum, and featuring locking hasps and waterproof seals. I'd seen such cases in crime movies.

"I need you to take this case to Chicago."

I blinked. "Chicago?"

"Someone will be waiting to receive it. They'll meet you at the airport. You are to hand over the case and return home on the next flight."

"What's in the case?" I asked timorously.

The four henchmen stepped forward. Their arms left their chests. Their hands awakened. Their fingers twitched.

"That's not your concern," the grandmaster replied calmly.

"Unfortunately, I have a wife in a wheelchair at home. I am only able to leave for short periods of time. Travel is out of the question for me right now."

The grandmaster glanced up at his men again. One of them nodded in confirmation of my story.

"Why didn't anyone tell me this?" the grandmaster muttered.

"I'm honored you felt you could trust me and sorry to let you down," I said, easing my way out of the room in a sort of moving kowtow.

On the way home, I realized that, having been wowed by Kenpo's Asian heritage and effective fighting techniques, I had completely missed the fact that this particular organization was training couriers and enforcers for the Mob.

I feel lucky to have escaped my brush with such people. I closed my school not long after that. As far as I know, the organization is still in existence.

. . .

Teachers can be people from any walk of life, family members, tradesmen, salesmen, landscapers, or healers. They don't have to be professional educators. They don't have to be model citizens. They don't have to be sages, nor do they have to be perfect in any particular way. Lessons are available from any and all experiences and from any and all of the people around us. Once our minds are open, we can see the way of nature running through even those we judge to be deeply flawed. Those flaws, and our judgments, teach us much about balance and imbalance, about the restoration of *wuji*, and about the consequences of both wrong action and inaction. The lessons we learn from luminaries and masters who either betray us or let us down can be very nearly as painful and powerful as those we learn from lovers and friends but should never stop us from seeking to follow those who live naturally, and whose efforts seem most easily and gracefully effective.

. . .

The shaft of wheat growing taller than the rest is frequently the first to be cut down. When it comes to advancing our circumstances, we thrive when we put down roots in our communities rather than skating across the surface of the world. We do better when we don't prioritize seeking attention for ourselves, but rather seek to support the interests, well-being, and worthy work of those around us. We prove ourselves better by our deeds than by our words, all the while nourishing networks often invisible to the naked eye.

. . .

Altruism and cooperation, what ecologists call eusociality, are the cornerstones of success for the human species on Planet Earth; competition, while common in the natural world, is not. In Daoist terms, this means we cooperate in child-rearing, we share resources, and we take care of each other. This impulse is a rare one in the natural world; it is found in primates and in rat species, in termites and ants, and likely in cetaceans. It's so easy to forget this basic fact, to forget that we evolved to work together for our survival and the betterment of all in our cohort, our tribe, our species, and our world. This is Daoism in its quintessence, following the way of nature to a more harmonious life.

COMMUNITY AND SOCIETY

It is morally wrong to make high-level information available to
only those who can afford to pay for it. After providing shelter,
food, water, and community, what more important job does a
society have than to educate its citizens? Access to knowledge
must be a right in our society, supported by programs that
assure it is fairly distributed to every socioeconomic stratum.
Free college and absolute net neutrality, with free broadband
for all, are some of the basic obligations of government. In this
way, our population's full intellectual resources can be applied
to solving the problems of the world.

...

Our schools, academies, and universities have lost their way
and purpose. Where once they were the most unfettered of
environments—the most unrestricted, safe, and convivial
places for research, scholarly inquiry, creative expression,
rational discourse, and debate—our educational institutions
have now become Romper Rooms for entitled children
who have spent years locked inside a system that allows
for no seepage from the outside world and no strong
influence but conformity. Education today has little to do
with understanding, learning, or thinking, and more with
performance on standardized tests. Professors, teaching
assistants, deans, and other administrators have sadly become
nursemaids suffering the scourge of political correctness
(an element in the great undoing of our society), unwilling
or unable to stand up for the high principles that once drew
them to their calling. It is time we put aside test scores,
dump standardized curricula, and develop fresh new ways
to teach our children about the world and their place in it.

Magnet schools with alternative and avant-garde curricula, Montessori-like teaching methods (which teach children *how* to learn and instill in them a lifelong love of doing so), and a paradigm shift in what parents expect from the educational system are required if we are to get back on track and save the process of institutional intellectual inquiry.

• • •

Professional educators are poorly remunerated. Their status has slid down the societal pole until they are barely more respected than gravediggers or truck drivers. What does this say about the value we put on education, the very backbone of any advanced and realized society? Let's reallocate assets from sports and entertainment to education. Let's eviscerate the budgets of sports leagues and slash the salaries of players and performers. Let's pay generous salaries to outstanding teachers rather than batters and pitchers, news anchors and thespians. Wouldn't such a reallocation of resources send a message to young people that learning, sharing, and growing mean more than running and jumping for the entertainment of others, woodenly reading words off a teleprompter, or cleverly pretending to be something we are not? The hallowed notion that fiction must not contain messages, that, if we want to send a message, one should "call Western Union" is an embarrassment. Placing entertainment above morality, celebrity above compassion, and deception above consciousness is a good indicator of how and why we're in the mess we're in.

• • •

The surest way to geld the human imagination is to limit the amount of time people have to think freely. At best, doing so creates unhappy conformists and disempowered contrarians. At worst, it creates legions of the disenfranchised and depressed. Slotted in to demanding routines by bosses, teachers, and even well-intentioned but misguided parents, deep thinking becomes a rare opportunity. Systems and policies that allow leisure only to the wealthy and privileged divide our society and thus are at least a means of social control and at most an assault on human rights. We must resist such control starting in kindergarten. We must ban homework. We must legislate long recesses. We must eschew rigid, test-oriented curricula and instead embrace teaching that is congruent with the physiology of children (scheduling classes for teens in the evening rather than early morning, for example), which emphasizes independent thinking, freedom, and personal development. We must continue to resist overwork right into our adult lives. No great scientific discovery, philosophical realization, or brilliant creation was ever born of toiling like a drone and being treated like a slave. In our resisting we must be creative and clever, so as not to use force against force but rather to exploit the weaknesses in the lives and ideas of our overlords.

. . .

Basic research is at the heart of scientific advancement. It must be free to wander like a river, pursue tantalizing tidbits and leads, sometimes run into a granite wall but other times lead to a vast ocean of knowledge and understanding. Yet so many of our inquiries into the nature of life and the universe are funded by corporate and government entities. Sadly, this is *another* example of the fox guarding the henhouse. We just can't trust such organizations not to foist their own agendas upon results, peddle influence, and advance their own interests. Explicitly or implicitly guiding scientific investigation in the direction of profitable products, weapons, or tangible technology rather than fundamental understanding destroys the flow, limits the adventure, and reduces the chance we will make unpredictable, life-changing discoveries. The disease of corruption has plagued the infrastructure of authority since time immemorial and has never fit with pure intellectual inquiry. Let's make an end run around special interests and legislate for government grants devoid of strings and agendas. A keen curiosity about the world and a desire to understand it better is fundamental to our nature. Let's make basic research basic again.

. . .

Evolution is the branch of science that most clearly defines who and what we are. It is closer to being our master and creator than any of a million gods we have concocted over our brief spasm here on Earth. It is important to understand that placing human beings in their rightful context of billions of years of life on this planet elevates the wonder of life and humanity rather than degrades it. To continue to embrace religious cosmogonies is an insult to the true beauty of nature. Religious fundamentalists who deny evolution retard, hamstring, and even insult the hard work of those incandescent minds striving to understand the world using the increasingly sharp lens of science. Teachers and schools who impugn evolution by calling it a theory are sucking mud through a straw and should be compassionately given a glass of clean water.

. . .

We have already begun to create life. Soon we will be creating it at a significant level of complexity and sophistication. Whether android or chimera, the new life forms with whom we will shortly share our world will challenge our ethics and morals and stretch the very definition of what it means to be alive. Judging by how we've done with animals and, frankly, with each other, the future of these beings does not look bright. Let's start thinking now about how we want to define ourselves in our interactions with our own intellectual spawn. Could we hold ourselves to a higher standard in how we treat our creations so they may come to see us as benevolent friends and neighbors rather than genocidal monsters and masters? Super AI is likely to judge us mercilessly.

...

China's last dynasty, the Qing, collapsed because of natural disasters, economic failures, and China's dwindling influence on the world stage. By the end of the nineteenth century, Japan and major nations of the West had so ruthlessly thrust their fingers into the Chinese pie that the original dish had lost much of its taste and shape. As has so often been the case throughout world history, these incursions were as much financial as military. China tried to fight back but it was insufficiently organized and capitalized and its weapons were primitive and inadequate. An ugly (and now ironic) saying arose: "China is the weak man of Asia."

Chinese people felt understandably disempowered, disenfranchised, and poorly used by invaders. Popular sentiments against foreigners grew and the people organized themselves against foreign incursions. One of the organizations was an evolved version of a secret society known as the Yihequan (Moral, Harmonious Fist). Ironically, this group had originally formed in opposition to the very Qing dynasty it was now supporting because Qing rulers were from a multi-ethnic northern tribe known as Manchus seen as non-Chinese. These Manchus, by the way, were descended from the Jurchens, who had formed their own "foreign" dynasty, the Jin. The Yihequan was populated primarily by young men, many of them peasants from the northeastern province of Shandong.

Foreigners referred to these nationalists as "Boxers" because they were devoted to martial arts and spiritual practices. Related to some of the disciplines I myself enjoy and teach, these pursuits built a sense of community, drew new followers, and led the rebels to become strong, capable fighters. A fiction arose that the exercises made them invulnerable to bullets. Even members of the Qing aristocracy were said to have fallen prey to this nonsense.

By the spring of 1900, Boxers were roaming the streets of Beijing. They committed acts of violence against foreigners, burning churches and homes and murdering non-Chinese in the streets. Their movement gathered enough momentum for Dowager Empress Cixi to issue a proclamation supporting them. Military campaigns on Chinese soil began between foreign legions and the imperial army. Despite this, the balance of power had not substantially changed and things did not go well for the Chinese. Forces from Britain, France, Austro-Hungary, Russia, Italy, and the USA descended upon the capital city. More than one hundred thousand people died before foreign dominion was restored.

Despite heavy losses, the rebel group continued to evolve and grow, until the communists came to power in 1949. Some of their offshoots and descendants continued to hold underground meetings wherein they now planned for a democratic rebellion. Others became the Chinese secret societies known as Triads and Tongs in the West. At the start, these latter were dedicated to protecting ethnic Chinese from persecution when large numbers came to America for railroad jobs and gold mining. They arbitrated disputes among locals in the traditional Chinese way, too. Every American Chinatown had some version of these groups, which later became primarily criminal organizations.

In a veiled reference to the Boxer Rebellion, my martial arts grandmaster once commented, "Some people thought kung fu was stronger than bullets. Those people are all dead now." One takeaway is that, as we evolve away from nationalism to globalization and thence to a higher version of our species—perhaps even into cyborgs with unimaginable physical powers and intelligence—ethnic pride, a sense of community, and righteous indignation may still be required before the yoke of tyranny can be broken. All the same, if we're going to rebel, we have to do so effectively, cleverly, and without self-delusion.

CHAPTER FOUR

CULTURE, COMMERCE, GOVERNMENT, AND POWER

C an one be both a Daoist and a patriot? The answer is a resounding yes. To do so, we have only to see the themes and trends within our country that are moving society toward the ideals we see as the best and highest—in my case, the ideas espoused in this manifesto—and spread and support them. This kind of high-mindedness, idealism if you must, is not found in divisive politics, nor in racism, greed, or corruption. Certainly, it is not present in the self-aggrandizing behavior of many leaders. It is likewise absent from partisanship, identity politics, rabid nationalism, and religious fundamentalism. To those who would accuse me and this work of being an Eastern version of the latter, I answer that you are welcome to put any label you like upon the way nature works, upon doing things that make logical sense, upon acting with sensitivity and compassion towards all sentient beings, and upon treating all non-renewable natural resources respectfully.

The intersection between Daoist thinking and politics appears not only in the workings of the awakened mind but also in the practical, external application of Daoist principles to everyday living, including the larger tasks at hand. Politics, in aggregate, is the name for such tasks. Politics are about conflict resolution, no matter how abstruse their proceedings may appear. At root, politicking is always about who will prevail and get what he or she wants. Steal from Peter to pay Paul. Work the middle ground. Develop a constituency. Serve the electorate. Be a populist, snollygoster, reformer, ideologue, demagogue, or a woman of the people. All these are just political lingo for being good enough at building bridges for a majority of potential supporters to want you in the game.

But how do we effect the change we want when it appears to be such a momentous task? The Daoist answer is that we don't meet obstacles head-on but rather flow around them.

Nature turns every conflict into a spiraling kiss. As mentioned at the outset, we see this example everywhere, from the way water goes down the drain to the way galaxies clashed in the aftermath of the Big Bang, when all matter was zooming away at unimaginable velocity from the primordial point, and everything that had been was condensed into a space smaller than the tip of a pencil. In this mad rush, this frenzied, chaotic flight from the center, collisions were happening constantly, and they were all resolved with spirals. In nature, meeting force with force is taboo.

. . .

Some years ago, a week before Christmas, I was in the drive-through lane at Starbucks. It was first thing in the morning, and the cars were lined up, bumper to bumper. When I reached the menu board, I recognized the barista by her London accent, and asked for a cup of tea. I was waiting for the cars in front of me to move up when the driver of an SUV behind me, apparently dissatisfied with the alignment between his lips and the order microphone, laid on his horn, leaned out his window, and shouted, "Move up, you idiot."

There was, of course, nowhere to go. Embarrassingly enough, my first reaction was to exit my vehicle and send him to the dentist for a holiday visit. "I'll teach you not to honk at strangers," I thought. Reaching for the door handle, I saw him in my side-view mirror. His face was red and twisted, and his eyes bulged. Catching a glimpse of myself, I realized I looked very much the same. Whatever his affliction, I had apparently contracted it. My anger melted away.

When I reached the payment window, I told the barista I wanted to buy the honker a cup of coffee.

"But he's an arse," she protested, having heard the entire exchange through the menu microphone.

I shrugged. "Probably just having a bad day. Who knows what's going on in his life? Maybe he just found out his wife cheated on him or his kid is sick. Maybe he got fired or lost his house."

"The problem is, he's buying breakfast for his entire office. It's a big order and a big bill."

I looked at my wallet. As is so often the case, it only contained a few dollars. I handed over my credit card.

"Are you sure about this?" she wanted to know.

"Just do it before I change my mind."

Driving away, I felt great. My anger had fled. I was happy and relaxed. I went on to teach a few tai chi lessons in the park and didn't return home until mid-afternoon. When I did, I found my answering machine so full it could not accept any more messages. Puzzled, I hit the "play" button. The first few messages were from the British barista, asking me to call the store. The next few were from the store manager. My first thought was that the credit card was no good. I kept listening. The next messages, a group of them delivered in urgent tones, were from a reporter for NBC News. He asked that I return his call at once. This plea was repeated over and over. As I was listening, my phone rang. I answered it. It was the reporter again.

"I'd like to come to your house," he said.

"What is this all about?"

"Were you at Starbucks this morning?"

"Are you kidding? This is about me buying coffee for a stranger?"

"More than just coffee."

"If you want to do a story about philanthropy, I'm sure you can find better material. There are people helping each other all over the world. Billionaires are sharing their fortunes. I'm not your man."

"I beg to differ. What you don't understand is that you did what you did at 8 a.m this morning and it is now 3 p.m. and people are continuing to buy coffee for the people behind them."

"That is interesting," I said. "But it might just be a marketing ploy by Starbucks."

"If it is, you started it. Are you sure I can't come to your home?"

"I'll meet you at the coffee shop," I said.

On camera a few minutes later, I explained to him that what he wanted to characterize as a holiday gift of random kindness was actually an act of consciousness, and it wasn't the least bit random. I told him how much Daoism prizes keeping one's emotional cool. I explained that, in any conflict, we can choose one of three doors. The first is to meet force with force, such as responding to the honk by yelling with a fist to the teeth. Not a great option. The second is yielding. I might, in the coffee case, have gotten out of my car, apologized for not moving up five inches, and offered to spit shine the honker's windows and wheels for him. Also, not the greatest choice. Door #3, I explained, is doing whatever it takes to regain one's equilibrium without opening either of the first two doors.

"But what is Door #3?" he wanted to know.

"Not Door #1 and not Door #2. A creative solution that is unique to each and every situation. Being able to figure it out is one of the goals of Daoist training. This morning, I chose to buy breakfast for

a stranger. In another circumstance, I would likely do something entirely different."

The story was popular enough to be covered in national news. It went online and around the world. I received quite a bit of email about it from friends around the globe, and from strangers, too. It was a great lesson for me regarding the power of a tiny act of no apparent significance. Our actions, it turns out, really do spread like waves, affecting others quite some distance away.

ASSUMING RESPONSIBILITY

One cannot simultaneously love freedom and eschew protest and activism. Rolling over for authorities, disappearing into the screen on the desk, sticking our fingers in our ears, and chanting to keep out the sounds of the world will not contribute to an open and fair society. Shunting poverty, homelessness, and drug addiction down the street with a not-in-my-backyard attitude is no way to deal with either adversaries or palpable human need. We have become a nation of sheep, afraid to stand up for what we know is right, afraid to risk anything, and content with the lot we have while turning a blind eye to the suffering of the world. When the people abstain, those in power become more powerful. It is time to shed our wooly coats and become wolves. It is time to devour greed, injustice, intolerance, the rape of the environment, and religious fundamentalism in one enormous gulp, time to digest them, and time to excrete them as fertilizer for the new world.

. . .

Why do we so often abandon our responsibilities to others, particularly to those in positions of authority? Why do we withhold our vote from the best candidate for a position when we don't believe that candidate can win? If cynical laziness can so easily lead us away from doing our duty, then perhaps we don't deserve the privilege of citizenship. Just because someone else thinks something is okay doesn't mean we should be doing it. If we are aware that something is wrong, it is our right and responsibility to oppose it even if that opposition requires civil disobedience. Let's be willing to deny the authority of any agency, government, or system that functions in an obviously immoral fashion.

. . .

When and where in our evolution did hominids, able to stand on two legs, survey the world and create our own environment that devolved into a toxic mass of uncaring humanity? When did we start to embrace such axioms as "that's just the way things are," "I live in the *real* world," "idealism is for losers," "time to face the music," "it is what it is," "wake up and smell the coffee," and "dreamers starve, workers thrive"? When did we abandon morality and philosophy only to loathe ourselves, become satisfied with eating hotdogs, commit genocide, suffer ill health, and embrace war and destruction? How did we become beasts who proclaim their wealth with houses, cars, jewelry, and T-shirts, all the while ignoring our starving, struggling sisters and brothers, and the countless sentient but invisible beings whose lives we take every day? The answer may be in the evolution of empires, which grow uncaring and decadent right before they crumble. Empires are nothing more than each one of us, magnified. Recognizing negative thoughts and actions for what they are, we can separate ourselves from

them and begin to relax and re-evaluate what we have taken
for granted thus far.

· · ·

Government must exist in a state of vibratory balance,
thrumming like a thick string at the input of the various
branches, always in search of a harmonious tone. In the face
of disharmony, totalitarianism grows like a tumor. The Fourth
Estate (the press) is essential if we are to avoid the cancer of
autocracy. Rather than assaulting reporters, an ominous sign
of burgeoning totalitarianism, let's celebrate a free and vibrant
press. Let's relish the sound of dissenting opinions as we would
harmonies sung behind a beautiful melody. Let's fight hard
against censorship, for it is the first tool of oppression. At
the same time, we must recognize that most of today's media
messages are born to advertise products, entertain us into a
stupor, or win over our opinion in the confidence game of
politics. Let's prize true journalism above the crown jewels
and point out journalistic biases. Let's become hypersensitive
to feeling self-righteous, beleaguered, entitled, or special. Let's
apply my special neologism "rectolalia" (meaning to speak
from the excretory orifice) to commercial media content.
Spread the word!

· · ·

Rather than choosing as our leaders strident celebrity
ideologues whose greatest interest is the size of their bank
account and whose greatest addiction is to adulation, why not
pick those who prefer a low profile to fame and who work
selflessly, tirelessly, and mysteriously to better our world?
A bad leader is one everyone hates. A better leader is one
everyone loves. The best leader is one who remains utterly

unknown to the public at large, while toiling all the while for the benefit of all. This is the person who has done the hard work on herself before committing to selfless service. Strutting, preening, and angling for personal gain have no place in government.

Ruling a great state
is like cooking a small fish
when you govern the world with the Tao
spirits display no powers
their powers do people no harm
the sage does people no harm
and neither harms the other
for both rely on Virtue

—Laozi Stanza 60[4]

---

4   Red Pine, *Lao Tzu's Taoteching*, 2nd ed., Mercury House: San Francisco, 1996.

• • •

*Many historians consider the Tang Dynasty (618–907 CE) to be
China's most illustrious period. Its capital, Chang'an (now called
Xi'an), was arguably the center of the Eastern world, with the famous
silk roads to the West beginning and ending there. What a glorious
time and city this was! Burgeoning commerce supported an array
of goods and services, and contact with the rest of the world fueled a
flowering of philosophy, art, and social reform. Tea drinking, already
popular, became a sophisticated pastime. Civil service was linked to
education and achievement and, for the first time, important posts
were filled by competitive examination, rather than nepotism or
influence-peddling. Literature bloomed, with new forms of prose
arising along with some of the world's most magnificent poetry,
particularly in the wilderness tradition (a personal favorite of mine).
While Buddhism gained traction during the Tang, Daoism remained
the era's dominant religion.*

*The cycles that Daoists study include the rise and fall of individuals
and societies. Yang gives rise to yin, which gives rise to yang again.
When a civilization reaches the kind of heights seen during the
Tang, we can be certain that revolution, collapse, and chaos will
follow. While the first half of the dynasty featured a strong central
government (albeit punctuated by usurpations, poisonings, and
overthrows), the latter half was rife with rebellion and the gradual
disintegration of centralized rule. Challengers to the emperor's power
arose, were quelled, and arose again. Excessive wealth and power led
to excessive behavior and consequent uprisings.*

*Perhaps the most famous of these, the An Lushan Rebellion (755–763
CE), came at the very pinnacle of the dynasty, at a time of both
tumult in the imperial court and great unrest in Eurasia. The
rebellion was supported by Arab, Sogdian, and Uighur groups (these
latter are the same Muslim people who resist the Chinese government*

*today in Xinjiang province) and lasted through the rule of three
emperors. The initial target of the action was the sitting emperor,
Tang Xuanzong. While Xuanzong was in some ways an enlightened
ruler who made things better for the people, stabilized the economy,
and abolished the death penalty, he also made some poor choices. One
was to put too much trust in a chancellor whose aggressive foreign
campaigns stimulated the revolt against him. Another was to become
utterly besotted by perhaps the most famous—some say notorious—
courtesan in Chinese history, Yang Gui Fei.*

*Born Yang Yuhuan, daughter of a provincial official, Yang was one
of several sisters. She was a beautiful girl, her looks so celebrated that
she is still considered to be one of the four most beautiful women in
Chinese history. One legend about her says that even flowers closed
in shame in her presence, while another claims she bathed endlessly
to stay beautiful. At fourteen, Yang was married to one of Xuanzong's
sons, thus becoming a princess. Naturally, the emperor attended
the wedding.*

*History would have unfolded differently had the emperor not caught
sight of his new daughter-in-law. Xuanzong became instantly
infatuated. He took her away from his son and sent her to a Daoist
temple for training, presumably in the arts of love. She became a nun
there and was given the religious name Taizhen. When her training
was finished, she entered the imperial court as Xuanzong's concubine.
He awarded her the title Gui Fei, signifying a previously unheard-of
level of prestige and power, along with enough gifts of gold and jewels
to make her a very rich woman. He even gifted her a famous hot
spring so she could bathe in comfort during the cold winter months.*

*One story has her asking him to fill a palace lake with wine so she
could bathe in it (he did, ordering his vassals to drain it and refill
it with countless thousands of barrels of spirits), while another has
her favoring lychee fruits, which her powerful patron had brought*

in from far-off orchards so she could enjoy them throughout the year. Other tales tell of her throwing tantrums, refusing her lover's attentions, and in other ways utterly and completely controlling him. Some versions of history have their love affair as one of the most compelling and romantic stories in the annals of Asia.

You can imagine how the other women at court felt about her, and you can imagine, too, how the emperor's infatuation affected the governing of the country. Utterly preoccupied with her, he failed to see trends, forestall plots, predict events, and ultimately stave off disaster. General An Lushan, architect of the rebellion that finally toppled Xuanzong and upended the dynasty, was in fact one of Yang Gui Fei's favorite military men and may have even had an inappropriate relationship with her. The chaos in court revolved around Yang Gui Fei like a solar system around a sun, with all motion catalyzed by an emperor who could control neither his appetites nor his empire.

When it all fell apart, thousands were dead, the capital was in ruins, the emperor was banished, and a new one was installed. An Lushan demanded the death of Yang Gui Fei. Some sources say she was strangled by an assassin while others record that she took her own life. The deposed emperor attempted to have her body recovered to be buried in a place of his choosing, but Gui Fei's remains were never found. Her disappearance, even after death, only added to the mystery of her life and love, inspiring countless operas, books, and films.

If ever there was an example of the effects of one person's personality and action upon a nation, this is it. It says a thing or two about Daoist amorous arts as well.

. . .

When politicians set different standards for morality in their public and private life in order to succeed, they create an atmosphere of jaded cynicism and undermine our trust in government. Let us hold our leaders to the highest possible standard, and legislate term limits on every position, no matter how lofty. In this way, we remind office holders that they are in service, create consequences to malfeasance, and avoid a degradation of civil society.

. . .

Civilizations live and die in cycles. They achieve great heights, then plummet to such morally reprehensible, unbalanced, and disharmonious depths of government tyranny and material excess that violent collapse soon follows. Despite the opportunity to learn from our errors, it does appear that human beings are doomed to repeat them over and over again. Rather than wait for the inevitable revolution and implosion we are facing, why not study ancient history, literature, and art for clues on how to avoid the mistakes of yore? Freedom of speech and expression (though not, of course, when the expressions are exhortations to violence or declarations of hatred) are bedrocks of a balanced and healthy society. Let's speak up, and when someone tries to shut us down, speak up about that, too. Why not start legislating now for equable distribution of social and environmental resources? Rather than emphasizing individual abundance, we might consider focusing our material benefits on the village, as was the case when we lived closer to nature. Instead of thinking only of our own circumstances and only of the short term, let's take the broad and long view. Wise decisions will result, and beneficial and efficient actions, too. The sooner we implement this change, the greater the chance we can avoid bloody social upheaval.

. . .

To be politically conservative means to be invested (often financially) in maintaining the status quo. To be politically liberal has lost its original streak of compassion and has become more about being self-righteous. Both liberal and conservative positions have become more about pedaling influence than spreading ideology. At both ends of the spectrum, politicians spin policies that relentlessly exploit the poor, wantonly destroy the environment, and engage in profligate and insensitive squandering of resources. This path to the breakdown of both planet and society must be countered by a real paradigm shift. As wishful as such a shift may sound, it is not only possible, it is necessary. To accomplish this, we only have to focus on harmony, balance, compassion, humility, and frugality.

. . .

My great-uncle, Herbert Henry Lehman served the state of New York as both governor and senator. He was also Director-General of the United Nations Relief and Rehabilitation Administration, and close associate of U.S. President John Fitzgerald Kennedy. Even though he died when I was just a little boy, I have many clear and fond memories of him. Among these is the time he told me that politicians must always live according to the highest possible standards because their lives were subject to constant scrutiny and they set the example for those they served.

Sunday brunch at Uncle Herbert's duplex apartment in Manhattan was a regular thing for our family. The great man sat at one end of a long table, his wife, my Aunt Edith, at the other. I remember wood paneling in the room, doilies on the table and sideboards, and Uncle Herbert's shiny head reflecting the light from the chandeliers above us. We typically ate lamb chops with mint jelly, or pork chops and limp asparagus enlivened by a silver tureen of hollandaise sauce, with mashed potatoes on the side. Dessert was some kind of meringue concoction, like Floating Island or Baked Alaska. Brandy was consumed in big glass snifters, while white and red wine bottles graced the table. My father swirled the wine in his glass, sniffing it before sipping. I remember there were always boxer dogs around, and, in his last years, a dusky gray, lion-cut poodle named JJ.

The last time I saw Uncle Herbert was the Sunday just after JFK was assassinated. I sat close to him, as I liked to do, and noticed that he didn't eat. In fact, his bald pate looked a bit stubbly that day, and his forehead bore a depression from resting on his empty plate during most of lunch. I didn't understand how fervently my uncle had believed in Kennedy's Camelot, how tirelessly he had worked for Kennedy's campaign, and how he saw him—through glasses permanently stained by World War II—as the last, best hope for the free world. Even as a first grader, however, I could tell something was wrong with Uncle Herbert.

The strangest thing to me about that day was how everyone just continued eating and talking, albeit in hushed tones, as Uncle Herbert remained in his downed position throughout the meal. It wasn't as if they hadn't noticed. It would have been easier to ignore Godzilla on a Lazy Susan. The lunch went on anyway, with people passing food and maids walking in and out with silver trays. I remember being served a lamb chop, its bone wrapped in white paper that ended in a puffy, folded hat.

Suddenly, Uncle Herbert lifted his head and looked down the length of the table at his wife.

"Someone shot JFK," he said, his voice barely a whisper but somehow cutting through every other sound in the room.

"Someone did, dear," replied my aunt.

"How could that be?"

"I don't know."

"I don't want to live in a world where someone would shoot JFK."

Aunt Edith gave no answer to that, and indeed there was none to give. There was, however, a comment available, and I made it, a few hours later, on the way back to our own apartment.

"Mom," I said.

"Yes?"

"Uncle Herbert's going to die."

A week later, while getting dressed to travel to Washington, DC, to receive the Presidential Medal of Freedom, Uncle Herbert dropped dead in his bathroom.

The times I most regret not having had more time with him are the times I yearn to hear his opinions on the politics of Daoism. I wonder whether he would have preferred the laissez-faire *politics of the great Daoist sage, Laozi, or the highly ordered and structured vision of Laozi's putative student, Confucius. Having been a liberal Democrat, I suppose Uncle Herbert would have very much liked the way Laozi saw the role of the king and court, namely to keep the people happy. At the same time, he might have found the great sage's emphasis on an ignorant populace objectionable, even if the rationale for keeping people in the dark was that they were happier that way.*

I'm certain Uncle Herbert understood the importance of a stable society. I know he would have grasped the appeal of Confucius's rules and social constructs, too. At the same time, I bet he would have chafed at the loss of freedoms that Confucianism entails and would have been aghast at the diminished role women played in the Confucian universe. As someone who understood the reality of politics and accomplished much on the world stage, Uncle Herbert, I bet, would have been very receptive to the Daoist argument that rules and relationships, like regimes, are changeable and fluid things. I believe he would have liked the way Daoist philosophy emphasizes never pushing too hard as, from what I gather, my uncle was big on respecting the opinions of others and knew better than to railroad anyone into anything. I think he would have also appreciated Laozi's emphasis on effectiveness without wasting energy. Nobody who accomplished so much and lived so long could really have lived any differently.

I would like to think that, over the fullness of time, I might have gained enough of my uncle's respect that he would listen to my explanation of the relationship between Confucianism and Daoism, and come to see them as yin and yang, as two sides of the same coin. I would hope he could see his way to recognizing the value of societal roles—especially the mutual respect between leader and led—while embracing a prescription for politics in which the external moral landscape found its blueprint in the values, priorities, and beliefs of the individual citizen.

. . .

Human organizations, whether political or religious, represent perhaps the greatest and most existential of all threats to human freedom and existence. Too often, they either impose the will of the few on the many, sacrifice freedom for ideology, or both. This is a perversion of the purpose of government, which is to provide infrastructure for the external expression of a moral conscience. Accordingly, government must protect the lives of all sentient beings, manage and preserve the environment and its natural resources, provide food, housing, education, and healthcare for all, defend the interests of minority groups, and integrate the governed population into the larger world community. All this must be done with maximum transparency, the lightest possible touch, and the greatest delicacy and care. It must be done, as Laozi says, in the way we would fry a small fish.

MORAL IMPERATIVES

Mistaking a person's salary for their personal value is a perverse assault on morality. It traces its roots to early civilizations, intensified during the Industrial Revolution, and since then has been tuned to a fevered pitch in a society that depends upon consumption for survival. Money is a word to describe the flow of energy between human beings; economics is a thin and brittle branch of psychology and is about as reliable as voodoo. To base a life on the pursuit of money is to engage in a form of group delusion. Measuring how rewarding work is based only on financial remuneration demeans human creativity and imagination. Considering human beings as financial assets strikes at the core of what is wrong with material society. To use a human being as a tool for profit is like using a cotton ball to turn a screw. Let's redefine a person's contribution to society in terms of his or her compassionate actions towards others and his or her work to benefit a dying planet. In doing so, we reap the simultaneous benefits of happier and more content individuals, a culture that recognizes the importance of helping each other, and a society that focuses on the future of our world.

• • •

Wealth inequality is the single most egregious problem in the human world today. When slightly less than a billion people are either hungry or food insecure, unbridled capitalism and unregulated markets exist only to keep the rich and powerful in position. Currently, the top 1% of the population holds as much wealth as the remaining 99% percent combined. The existence of the super-rich is not only disharmonious and unbalanced, it is frankly outrageous, a sign that we have greedily interfered with the natural, global flux Daoism describes for all energy and resources, one that keeps resources from being concentrated in just one place or with one group for more than a short period of time. Who, exactly, is creating this imbalance by interference? Scofflaws who believe rules are not for them, flaunt taxation (which they regard as robbery), disdain governments (which they regard as corrupt), ignore international borders (which they see as no more than minor annoyances when traveling by private jet or yacht), and focus solely on lining their own pockets. In a circular bit of faux reasoning, such international conmen claim redistribution of wealth kills personal initiative when, in fact, living with wealth out of reach does more to demotivate the poor than anything. The hugely rich should be reduced to menial jobs and their cash reserves (in certain cases more than the gross domestic product of small countries) allocated to social programs worldwide. Redistributing wealth through any and all peaceful means will free up funds for the social programs so critical to restoring the world. It must begin now. Redefining success in the direction of personal development rather than social status or material gain will tip our economy in the right direction. Imagine the healing, balancing wave that would occur if each and every one of us dedicated ourselves to the task.

. . .

We have a minimum wage, but it lags behind inflation, perpetuates poverty, and guarantees nothing. Those who say there are no guarantees in life haven't paid taxes and haven't been to a funeral. In a civilized society, we need not only a minimum wage and unconditional minimum income but an income ceiling as well. Without these regulations, we remain mired in a zero-sum model, wallowing around in the mud of free enterprise, valuing the least important things in life, all the while ignoring the dignity and needs of our brothers and sisters and children, too. The sooner we shift our paradigm to disentangle self-worth from net worth, the more prepared we will be for the coming robotics revolution which will render the very concept of work obsolete and leave vast swaths of our society economically useless. We need to start valuing ourselves and each other for who we are, not what we earn. Compassion trumps capitalism every time.

. . .

Hunger, like poverty, stands against *Dao*. Resources must flow from those with the most to those with the least. Ending hunger is not something we should relegate to a few non-governmental organizations. Every one of us has both an opportunity and an obligation to help the hungry in our own community and across the globe. Starvation cannot stand. If we see a hungry person, we must feed her. What could be simpler? What say we all donate time to soup kitchens? What say we vocally and financially support national lunch programs for students of all ages and contribute to, and legislate for, home delivery of meals to the elderly and infirm? Let's bring moderation to our behavior around food and pay more attention to how much we eat and how much we waste. Let's not grocery shop when we're hungry. Let's buy only what we will actually consume. Let's store food items individually in

metal or glass rather than in plastic. If we find ourselves with
more than we can eat, let's share what we can with the needy.

• • •

When we make investments, whether in the form of time,
money, or labor, let's be sure we know what we are investing
in and support its principles, effects, conditions, and
consequences. Projects that benefit only ourselves are suspect.
Even more so are corporations, ventures, and associations
whose values are not nurturing and conscious. Business
enterprises are a reflection of the principal players and, people
being as they are, may be more about greed than generosity,
more about short term gain than long term benefit, and more
about taking advantage of others than about supporting
compassion and growth. Why not choose our projects wisely,
not only so they don't come back to bite us later but also
because the more our actions resonate with our philosophies,
the better we can leverage our efforts? Our investments
reflect upon us. The more congruent they are with the Three
Treasures of compassion, humility, and frugality, the more
effective and meaningful they will be.

• • •

We have forgotten that the purpose of business is to generate
jobs that actually provide value to individuals and society,
create products, and provide services for our communities.
Business exists for us to help each other have a better life, not
to abuse and control each other, not to strive to be at the top
of the heap and tread others underfoot, and most certainly
not to value profit so highly that we are willing to cut costs
by eliminating human beings in favor of cheap, artificial
substitutes. Profits must be distributed first to employees,

second to company development, third to social programs, and lastly to investors. We must enact legislation prohibiting the profit of replacing people with robots, except in the case of jobs no human being desires.

...

In the 1980s, after leaving veterinary school to care for my ailing wife, I was making a meager living teaching martial arts and penning newspaper ads in Southern California. One day, an opportunity to write a corporate brochure for a nutritional products company came my way. I'd never had such a client before and saw the work as a good way to pay down my wife's medical bills. The company was pleased with the job I did and sent me more assignments. They continued to be happy and the work poured in. After pursuing this arrangement for some months, I was invited to attend the company's annual sales meeting in Texas. I responded that my wife was ill and that I could not travel. By way of reply, they sent tickets for us both, and arranged for away-from-home care for her.

Before the big bash, I spent time touring the company offices. I met the folks I'd been working with over the phone, putting faces to names. I came to some unflattering conclusions about the level of competence of some folks in the organization but I held my counsel. Their effective products were formulated by a Nobel-prize-winning chemist, they were helping people, and I was helping the sales force raise interest in them. At the big meeting, I was brought up on stage and thanked for creating such useful and high-quality sales tools.

The next morning, as I prepared for an early flight back to California, my hotel room phone rang. The company's chairman was downstairs, wanting to breakfast with me. I reminded him I was set to fly out in just a short while but he insisted we meet. We sat down over bagels and coffee.

"You're smart," he said. "I can smell it."

He went on to suggest that I move to Texas and work for the company onsite. I told him I was flattered but that I had a martial arts school in California and my wife's family was there. I thanked him very much for his business and emphasized how much I was looking forward to continuing to create great content for him. He did not take kindly to my refusal and pushed the point strongly. I repeated my position, again emphasizing how well it was working for both of us. The more I declined to move to Texas, the more strenuously he demanded I do so.

It didn't take long for me to realize that the chairman was not used to being denied, and that he was not going to take no for an answer. The more he pressed, the more I saw my job with his company evaporating. I wished it were otherwise but moving to Texas was neither logistically nor financially feasible. At last, angry at being pushed so hard and frustrated at seeing a lucrative arrangement go up in smoke, I told him that the reason I wouldn't move to Texas was that I had met all his people and not one of them was smart enough to be my boss.

Realizing his arrogance had suddenly met its match in my own, I immediately regretted my words. I started to retract them but then he leaned forward, drilled me with his eyes, paused for a moment, and burst out laughing.

"I suppose that's true," he said. "How about if I make you the boss?"

He mentioned a salary beyond the wildest dreams of a martial arts teacher and part-time copywriter. It was the proverbial offer and I could not refuse it. A week later, a moving van pulled up in front of my California apartment, and my wife and I were off to Texas.

The first year in the job was a whirlwind. I reorganized a big chunk of the company, hired the large staff I needed to do things right, and contributed to a truly dramatic increase in sales. The company was in the news for the allegedly controversial claims we were making about the antioxidant theory of disease—now reasonably well established but cutting-edge stuff back then—but the negative press seemed only to help us. I was aware that my boss was a dubious character but I turned a blind eye toward his foibles. The business was thriving and I was paying down my debts. I didn't want to rock the boat.

One night, working late at my operations office in the company warehouse, I heard noises coming from the shipping department. Unable to imagine who might be there at that hour and why, I went to investigate. I opened the door to find a team of men pitching pennies and drinking beer amidst cardboard boxes filled with bottles of our nutritional supplements but also with plastic bags of white powder. In a flash, I understood that one of my boss's henchmen was using our legitimate distribution network to ship illegal narcotics across the country. The men stared at me and I stared back. The standoff continued until I beat a tactical retreat, drove home, and slept with a revolver under my pillow.

First thing the next morning, I confronted my boss in his office. I told him I knew what was going on. He didn't appear the least bit surprised.

"We have a good and legitimate business here," I said. "We employ a lot of good people. They need and appreciate the work, and they're doing a great job. There's no need for extracurricular activities. You're making a fortune. Go sail the Caribbean in your yacht for six months. Let me clean this up."

"I have no idea what you're talking about," he replied.

"Either you put a stop to it or I will," I said.

He pulled a nail file from his desk drawer and became absorbed in a manicure. After a moment, he told me he knew people in New Orleans who could make me disappear. I countered by telling him I'd written a letter to the press and that a trusted friend had instructions to deliver it if I didn't show up the next day to retrieve it.

"I still don't know what you're talking about," he said.

"You know enough to threaten my life," I answered.

"You're fired," he said.

"I'm not leaving without a severance and your word you'll end it," I said. "I'll know. I have friends here."

It took a bit more negotiating but we came to an agreement. That night, still vibrating with fear from my game of brinksmanship, I again slept with a gun at hand. The next morning, I put my wife on a plane back to California, filled a trailer with things I cared about, and left town.

A few months later, as the result of an anonymous tip, the Texas State Attorney General conducted a raid. The company folded. Arrests were made. I was never questioned.

. . .

Agriculture potentiated human civilization, although recent archeological evidence shows that the quality of life people enjoyed in Paleolithic times outstrips our own in many ways. While there are arguments for both modern life and the pristine affluence of our early days, nothing can justify the unspeakable horror of industrial meat production.

Otherwise known as factory farming, this enterprise generates levels of cruelty no compassionate and awakened person can condone. The barbaric details of how such farms treat animals defy both digestion and comprehension and are thus avoided during mealtime. Factory farming, including dairy production, represents the typical profit-over-conscience approach of the large corporations that rule our world. Taking advantage of both peddled influence and the economies of scale, factory farming has nearly extinguished traditional farming methods, including the family farm. As if this were not enough, the pollution generated by factory farms has literally destroyed communities across the country. Perhaps worse, as a consequence of digestion, livestock turn grazing land into desert, creating dust, drying rivers, costing trees that are essential for CO_2 management and oxygen production, as well as producing the greenhouse gas methane, one of the underlying causes of ominous climate change. Supporting the small farmer, who must price her goods to purchase competitive technology, is the first step to bringing down Big Agriculture. In the end, however, the very best way to put factory farmers out of business is to simply stop eating beef, pork, chicken, and turkey.

. . .

It is not just sugar and dairy themselves that offend but also the companies that profit by producing these products that sicken us. Big Candy, Big Booze, and Big Soda are strong examples. How can a government that has the welfare of its citizens in mind allow the marketing of products that kill us? We went after tobacco but have kept away from products that contribute to the obesity epidemic. What are we thinking when we allow candy companies, soda businesses, and liquor manufacturers to aggressively market to a populace vulnerable to both their

seductive messages and to addiction? Sugar and alcohol are just
as addictive as tobacco, and yet their lobbies have succeeded
in keeping them free from prosecution. Isn't it time to stop
allowing people to profit from the illness and dependence
of others?

· · ·

The weak become prey in nature, yet it is the human being's
deepest triumph to transcend primitive instincts in favor of
compassionate morality. Crimes against the weak are among
the gravest of all moral transgressions, yet they are the crimes
that are most likely to be excused on the basis of cultural mores
or so-called natural tendencies. Whether we're talking about
forced marriages, slavery, financial abuse of disenfranchised
workers, sex trafficking, or child labor, taking advantage of
those with less power is a sign that we are self-indulgent, wont
to make excuses for our personal appetites and excesses, and
haven't learned much since the Stone Age. Bringing such vile
customs into the open is the first step toward legislating against
them. Voting with our pocketbooks is even more effective.
Let's boycott companies that use sweatshop labor and shine the
light of public opinion on all human rights abuses.

· · ·

Like racism, gender bias is often too subtle for the biased
person to notice and too thin and weak a presence to make
itself loudly known. It creeps in with assumptions, nicknames,
jibes, or, the worst case of all, unconscious indifference and
the ignorance of a human being. Let's make a meditation
out of reviewing the people in our lives, considering them
carefully and asking ourselves whether we truly regard them
without bias. Imagine how little need there would be for laws

and regulations if we just treated others as we would have them treat us.

. . .

Judging a consenting adult on the basis of his or her sexual preferences and activities is a sign of a weak mind. Such weakness can arise from a phobia, the pernicious influence of religion, or both. Sexually-based fears and prejudices have an evolutionary basis, but today, they are as useful and appropriate as gills on a camel. If our prejudices are a result of trauma, we need help. If they stem from religious fundamentalism, it is time to step away from our devotions and to cleanse ourselves of hateful thoughts. There is not now, nor has there ever been, room on Planet Earth for the kind of ignorant intolerance those practices breed. Only by opening our hearts and minds can we become capacious, sensitive, and kind.

WE AND THEY

Is empire-building acceptable in today's world? Is it really okay to wake up every morning asking who we bombed today? How have our corporate masters managed to convince us that brands and customers are worth the cost of perpetual war in a world where a billion people don't have enough to eat? Is there no end to our greed and hubris? Violence and strife may be a global reality, but still we must learn from—rather than conquer or profit off of—other countries. We must lend a helping hand across international boundaries, but only when that help is requested. Every time we are forced to take up arms, we must mourn the failure of our philosophy. Could we focus on the hunger, disease, and injustice within our own borders, please, and take better care of our wounded when they return from unavoidable, defensive conflicts?

. . .

Flags and borders invite separation from those not like us. They lead to intolerance and encourage the delusion that there are meaningful differences between us. They create separation rather than compassion, introduce ugliness where beauty could reign, and dupe us into believing that our petty differences are more than inch-high bumps and berms on the cosmic stage. While nation states and borders may be temporarily necessary as we move past tribalism, fanciful religious beliefs, and aggressive, self-aggrandizing behavior, it must be the ambition of every awakened person to see them erased. Biology trumps belief every time, and it is now a biological necessity to work together to keep our planet habitable for all. Let's replace patriotism and nationalism with idealism and utopianism.

. . .

The key political question is not, and perhaps has never been, the traditional East/West disagreement about whether individual rights trump those of society. Contrasting Eastern and Western cultures is an interesting intellectual exercise, but the real work is to elevate global consciousness to the point where every individual recognizes that the carbon in our bodies is the same as that in the stars, and that the water in our blood once ran through dinosaur veins. We must abandon the notion of the individual as a separate entity in favor of that of citizen of the world. In doing so, we realize that every acre fracked harms us all, every gallon of gas injures each of us, every yard of private waterfront deprives the rest of us, and every billionaire's portfolio is an atrocity.

. . .

The rights of indigenous people to practice their rituals, hold to their land, and maintain what is sacred to them has become a political flashpoint. How strange! What did we expect after we've built an empire by taking and killing? People who have been conquered, beaten, disenfranchised and reduced to third-class citizenry in a nation no longer theirs have very real grievances and heightened sensitivities. Building a telescope atop a mountaintop sacred to them or running an oil pipeline through a valley sacred to their ancestors is not merely adding insult to injury, it is a callous act and calamitous in and of itself. The same folks who deny native rights have no problem with their own right to own gas-guzzling cars or to make satellite-based space weapons. Granting dignity is the very least we can do for those we conquer.

The sage has no fixed heart and mind.
Therefore the hearts and minds
of ordinary people
become his.

To good people, he is good,
to those lacking goodness,
he is also good.

Virtue is good.

Truthful people, he trusts.
Those lacking honesty, he also trusts.

Virtue is honest.

In this world the sage
brings harmony to harmony,
universalizing
the hearts and minds of people.

People fix their eyes and ears.
The sage regards them as children.

—Laozi Stanza 49[5]

---

5   Sam Hamill, *Tao Te Ching—A New Translation*, Boston: Shambhala, 2005.

While the genesis of "strong" artificial intelligence may indeed be our ultimate purpose, being surveilled and controlled by both the state and the Internet is most assuredly not. If personal privacy has indeed been lost, it is only because we have become too fat, too happy, and too complacent about being manipulated by those who profit precisely from our complacency. If we buy mechanical things instead of electronic ones, both our security and our brain will benefit. Let's cover our computer's camera aperture and turn off every one of the GPS functions on our phones and tablets. Let's disable our car's navigation system and learn to use a map, a side benefit of which is a grasp of the big picture and global geography (something our younger generations lack). Let's deprive satellite-jockeying market researchers of any and all information about us. Let's employ security software to maintain our privacy online and thwart the commercial ambitions of Big Data miners.

. . .

The digital revolution is a totalitarian's wet dream. Using Big Data collection and consumer surveillance, the corporate world now has the tools not only to track our buying patterns but also to predict them. Digital profiling has become so subtle that our states of mind are there for interpreting by the attention economy, our political opinions obvious, and our secrets and other vulnerabilities available to be misused for blackmail or leverage. While the holders of these powerful tools may be convinced the authorities cannot and will not appropriate these tools for their own political aims, such convictions are naïve. As politics are subsumed by information, our individual identities become increasingly frangible. If this is not what we want, and Daoists do not, we must stand fast against the trend.

...

Millennia ago, we put ourselves at the apex of the pyramid
of life. In doing so, we felt better about hardship, loss, aging,
and death. This system served its purpose back then, and for
those who prefer to proceed with their fingers in their ears
and their eyes tied shut, it still does. Awakened people now
understand this age-old mythology to be nothing more than
fawning self-admiration. We are no better than the animals
with whom we share the planet; in terms of the way we destroy
our world, we are far worse. Using helpless animals as the
subjects for laboratory testing is beyond unconscionable;
it is criminal. Why not let companies know we care more
about the lives of rabbits than we do about having yet another
deodorant or lipstick in our bathroom chest? Let's exhort them
to use computer modeling in lieu of torturing chimpanzees
and monkeys. Let's stand against the needless suffering of
sentient beings.

...

*The more troublesome the nation's woes become, the more each of us
seems to complain about all the bad things "happening to me." The
distinction between "happening in the world" and "happening to me"
may seem specious, trivial, or even irrelevant, but in fact, it could not
be more important. Interpreting external events through our own eyes
is a necessary consequence of having eyes—indeed, of being human—
but interpreting events as aimed at you by some imagined God as
punishment is simply a road to misery. Pain, as the Buddhists say, is
inevitable, but suffering is optional.*

*Some of us are inextricably married to the idea that the world is
cruel and unfair, choosing to live in a judgmental, negative state that
separates us from others. Others, by contrast, disconnect from the*

world because we find it too painful, building emotional or physical walls to prevent people and pain from entering. Both these tactics bring little joy and require lots of energy. The good news is, there is a third option: to engage things more deeply and bring our passion, energy, and intelligence to bear on creating a wholeness that includes us (although it may not be controlled by us), while evidencing a harmonious interplay of opposing forces.

The sublime Chinese martial art of tai chi employs a game called "Pushing Hands" to teach us how to execute this third option—what I referred to earlier as Door #3. This game is cooperative rather than competitive. It must be practiced with a partner willing to keep her ego in check and eschew any agenda, save learning. It is best to engage this game, which is training for both the body and the mind, at an authentic tai chi school. Fortunately, the discipline is growing in popularity and there are classes everywhere these days.

The first stage of the game is to learn to keep our balance. To do this, we try to relax, offer no resistance, and feel light as a cloud in the torso, while sinking and rooting strongly with our lower body. We also learn how to grip the ground with our feet, turn our waist to deflect a partner's incoming force, and keep our spine straight, eyes leveled, and breathing smooth and easy. Of course, it is not only important to maintain balance in tai chi class. Without our own emotional and physical equilibrium, how can we respond to all that life dishes out? If we are angry, desperate, fearful, depressed, or falling down, we can't see clearly or act appropriately.

In the next level of Pushing Hands, we develop sensitivity by turning our fingers, palms, and forearms—eventually all parts of our bodies— into human ultrasound and x-ray machines. Using these tools, we sense our partner's intention before it becomes action. Cultivating such sensitivity requires our complete attention. If our mind wanders for a moment, we can lose track of what our partner is doing and *she may then take us off balance. Concentrating on the other person in our two-person world draws us out of our own dramas and expands the boundaries of our world. Imagine how such skills could enhance our empathy and compassion. Imagine what negotiators and diplomats we would all be if we were so sensitive to others.*

At the highest level of Pushing Hands, we lose the distinction between our partner and ourselves. Gone is the non-dual view of the world, and with it any notion of "other" or any compelling sense of "I." Gone are attachments to antagonism, preservation, agenda, reaction, or ego. When we achieve this level of practice, we come to realize that conflict is an attitude as much as a reality. Once we figure this out, Door #3 reliably presents itself. Does this third option require us to be passive? Does it obviate the possibility of evil or injustice in the world? Does it preclude the imperative that we should stand up for our own interests? No, no, and no. What it does do is give us a nuts-and-bolts way to both duck life's curveballs and, when we can't, to recognize that they are not deliberately aimed at us.

...

VIOLENCE AND THE USE OF FORCE

While I eschew mainstream gun culture and the very idea of using a gun to take the life of a sentient being, I very much enjoy the discipline and pleasure of precision target shooting. Punching paper or knocking down metallic silhouettes at a distance can be every bit as meditative a discipline as archery or the tai chi swordplay I have engaged daily for decades of my life. I've spent countless rewarding hours behind the sights with my finger on the trigger. I've learned much about stilling my breath, focusing my mind, and quieting my body for precision control.

There was one particular shooting experience so dramatic and inexplicable in any Newtonian terms that it demanded I transcend what I thought I knew and understood and opened me to a completely different reality. It occurred after a picnic with a group of friends along the high banks of a river. After we had finished eating, I produced a finely-made air pistol designed for ten-meter Olympic competition and took a few potshots at a bullseye I had inked into a cardboard box.

"Hey," said my host, pointing at a glint in the distance, across the ravine, clear on the other side of the river. "Looks like someone else likes plinking, too. Isn't that a Coke or Pepsi can tied to a tree?"

Squinting against the afternoon sun, I could just make out a spot of red. When a gust of wind came up, it moved.

"Could be," I allowed. "You can thread a line through the pull-tab. I did it lots of times as a kid."

"Give you a million dollars if you can hit it," he said.

"And if I can't?"

"Obviously you can't," he answered.

I took a wild guess and tilted the barrel upward. Everyone at the picnic gathered around me the way people do when someone is about to swallow an open penknife or wrestle a rabid Rottweiler.

"You know the spring in that gun can't send a pellet that far," someone said.

"You know it's a moving target, dangling like that," said someone else.

"You can't even see the damn target," a third person opined.

I tilted the barrel nearly skyward, thinking about trajectory and gravity, windage, and elevation. I knew there was simply no way to calculate them with an unpredictable wind and a pellet light as a feather. I closed my eyes when I took the shot, wondering about the nature of the universe and the power of mind and the concept of probability. I didn't even know I'd hit the can until I heard a tiny, distant "clink" and the roar of the assembled crowd.

"That's just not possible," said my challenger.

"I'm a millionaire," I smiled, my eyes still closed.

A week or so later, my paternal grandfather came to visit and I told him the story. I showed him the air pistol I'd used. He handled it carefully, checking to be sure it was empty, his thick fingers running over the smooth metal.

"I grew up in a small village in Russia," he said. "After the Russian Revolution, Alexander Kerensky came around with thugs to conscript us into the Red Army. He gave speeches. He was quite the talker but I didn't believe a word he said. I didn't want to die for him and his ideas so I sewed my fingers together. That way, I couldn't shoot a gun and wouldn't have to go to war. His so-called doctors ripped my fingers apart and drafted me anyway, telling me how lucky I was to be able to serve. I ran away and started a militia with my brother. Teenage boys from the village followed us. I was the leader. We smuggled guns across the border into Poland. Not toy guns like this. Real ones. Our father was a moneylender and war rifles came to him. Gold and jewelry, too. One day, when we were coming back from a run, we smelled smoke. I knew right away it was a pogrom."

"When the tsar sent his Cossacks, his Tatars, to make trouble for the Jews," I said.

He nodded. "They were terrific horsemen. Steppe people, you know. They lived on those horses. We did too, being smugglers. We got to the village and they had set fire to many houses. Raped women. Killed a few men who tried to fight back."

I could tell by watching his face that, in his mind, he was back in the world of his childhood. "We went after them," he said. "We knew the forest better than they did. Better than anyone. It was our job to hide, to know every tree. To know the shortcuts. We knew which way they'd be going and we got there first. We hid in the trees."

"Like Robin Hood," I breathed, feeling instantly stupid.

He shrugged. I don't think he knew the name.

"When they came through on their horses, we shot them. Even though we were just boys, they never had a chance. We buried them. It was hard work. Some of us wanted to keep the horses but it was too dangerous. Nobody else had horses like that. They'd be recognized and people would come looking. Of course, they came for us anyway. That was the end of that life for me. I became an outlaw. Because of my anger. Because we had guns."

"And then you met Grandma."

He nodded, slowly. "Again, guns. It was after the revolution. She and her family were in their summer house, a little dacha. They were hiding there even though it was winter. They had no food, really, but they had nowhere else to go. I was riding by on my horse and I saw two soldiers stop there. I watched. They went in. Your grandmother and her identical twin sister were there, both beauties. I watched through the window. Their parents were cultured people, her father a university professor, her brother a violinist, a musician. I was curious. Something drew me there. I watched through the window and the soldiers took down their pants and put your grandmother and her sister on the floor."

"I don't need to hear this," I said.

He waved away my objection. "I shot the first one from outside the house. The other one came out and ran. He didn't even try to mount his horse. I followed him. There was a railroad track not far away and he ran down the middle of it because the snow was thinner there. I shot him in the back."

I noticed then that my grandfather was crying. "In the back," he repeated.

I thought about how far things had come in just three generations, from shooting murderers and rapists to shooting cans of Coke. I thought about the trajectory of my family, from their days of trying to maintain their culture and survive against social pressures to my days, in another time and in another land, where I had the luxury of attempting to transcend the laws of physics with a pellet gun. I realized in that moment that, whether we like it or not, we define and understand our world in the context of those closest to us, and that our lessons and behaviors therein are a predictor of our regard for our larger social circle.

I went to the couch and gave my grandfather a hug.

He pushed the pellet gun off the couch and nudged it away with his foot.

...

Weapons are a necessary evil but should not be celebrated. Competence with the weapons of the day is justifiable—it remains critical to be able to defend ourselves against both tyrannical rule and society's malefactors—but a culture that condones violence and ignores its human cost is not. While the hard power of the club, axe, army, and gun can work in the short term, over time, it requires callousness, tough choices, and cruelty, all of which birth resistance, rebellion, and retribution. Soft power, by contrast, works more slowly, requires compassion, patience, and moral authority, and involves advancing the agenda of others as well as our own. Yet it is soft power that is more likely to build trust, engender loyalty, and foster friendships and alliances. The magnitude of the challenges we now face globally calls for long term solutions and thus for soft power. We must strategize accordingly, thinking generations and even centuries ahead. It's a new, smart paradigm for the millennium to come.

. . .

Random violence is the sign of a damaged mind and is incompatible with the survival of human life on Earth. In fact, the two kinds of violence—overt and physical, and covert and passive—feed each other in a never-ending dance. While some may argue that we are violent monkeys with violent genes, others argue that violence has all the hallmarks of a contagious disease, spreading itself, damaging its host, and being treatable. Either way, Daoism recognizes that, while violent behavior is sometimes required to bring things back into harmony and balance, it is always a last resort and always something to be mourned. Greed, lust, envy, moral outrage, and religious fervor may vociferously demand violence but are, in fact, better served by justice and compassion.

· · ·

Without laws, no rights and freedoms can be guaranteed and no nation can survive. Most law enforcement officers are well-intended professionals who put their lives on the line for the rest of us every day. Some are even extraordinary heroes. The law enforcement community, however, is no more or less likely to have a few bad apples than any other profession. One way we can help diminish corruption in law enforcement is to make sure, as some European countries do, that no officer serves in the town in which he or she was raised and that no officer serves in any one branch of service for more than a year. Respect officers' dedication and courage and support their efforts, but be wary of abuses of power. Film or record every meaningful encounter with law enforcement. Doing so may prove useful, should misunderstandings or conflicts arise.

· · ·

Broken windows policing, the practice of focusing law enforcement on minor street crimes and misdemeanors, is attractive in its simplicity. It is also fundamentally flawed. Crime, like the human mind, is complicated. Forcefully impressing order upon a fundamentally disordered system is futile. Why not recognize the need to make such an impression, and even any need to control other people, as being a sign of a fearful, insecure, and troubled mind? Let's accept that, in the world as it is, enforcing laws is necessary but not desirable, and work towards creating a society wherein our personal, moral code of conduct provides all the enforcement we need. Until we achieve that, let's turn our attention from people selling marijuana on corners to protecting the vulnerable, the weak, the sick, the elderly, and the innocent. Instead of profiling for petty transgressions, let's root out corruption in the world of high finance, representative government, and, of course, law enforcement.

· · ·

The militarization of police is a worrying trend. It is hard to know whether the entertainment industry is leading this development with films that glorify war, killing, weaponry, and militaria, or whether the movies are taking the lead from power-drunk enforcement agencies who envy the equipment and panache of their military cousins. Either way, seeing armored cars and tanks in the streets, and seeing planes, trains, and transportation hubs bristling with battlefield uniforms and weapons, is a sign that free societies are going extinct. It is past time to drop the GI Joe nonsense and fight crime by building relationships and trust between law enforcement and communities.

· · ·

The war against drugs is an outrage. It wastes precious resources on failed, ineffective, and unjust policies. Driven by special interests and conservative fearmongers, it has succeeded in building a stupendously expensive domestic and international law enforcement bureaucracy. It has put millions in jail on trivial charges and destabilized an entire continent. It has also inflated the price of product and made drug lords rich as kings. Last but not least, as a result of the stigmatizing of addicts, it has created a cohort of unsung victims—medical patients, in genuine need of pain relief—who are suspected of drug-seeking when they ask for it. Denying succor to those in agony on some specious, political basis is a moral outrage. If we legalize drugs and apply even a fraction of what we spend on interdiction to education, social programs, and government-funded rehabilitation, we can wipe out the suffering, crime, and tragedy of addiction, treating the latter as the disease that it is rather than as some failure of character.

. . .

The practice of torture lowers us to the level of those we are seeking to defeat. In addition to breaching a moral law higher than any law of our land, torture is also not particularly effective in gleaning accurate information. Captives under duress say whatever they think their captors want to hear. Given the technology at the disposal of our military and law enforcement today—from orbiting satellites able to read an outdoor café menu sitting in someone's lap to widespread surveillance using our wireless devices—there is no longer any reason to rend men's flesh and brutalize their minds in pursuit of information.

. . .

Only authoritarian regimes imprison people for their race, religion, political position, lifestyle choice, or commission of a misdemeanor crime. Such regimes, identifiable by their outsized prison population, have strayed very far from morality, cannot endure, and must be lawfully resisted and non-violently replaced. The fact that so many of our citizens are incarcerated is a sign that our society is sick; the large-scale practice of putting prisoners into solitary confinement for long periods of time is a greater sign of an even more profound illness. Primarily aimed at those who do not easily "fit into the system" or those whose mental illness makes them difficult to manage in a prison setting, victims of solitary confinement suffer long-term mental problems as a result of their isolation. That our society still engages in something this primitive as a form of punishment or control speaks to the hollow souls running our penal system. Let's put an end to solitary confinement today.

. . .

We call it the death penalty; previous cultures called it human sacrifice. Either way, study after study shows that it does not work as a deterrent to crime. Moreover, no system of justice can ever be perfect—eyewitnesses are notoriously unreliable, evidence can be tainted, and our standards of guilt and transgression change with time—a truism that has led to the execution of many innocents. Killing is intolerable. Killing the innocent is a horror beyond civilization. As if that were not enough, and it is, we have only to consider how often people who were once branded criminals later move to respected positions of power and prestige. History is full of examples of outcasts and revolutionaries who come to lead nations, and rehabilitated miscreants who become saints. None of this can happen if lives are taken. Now is the time to abolish the death penalty and to bring state-sponsored murder to a close once and for all.

. . .

Not quite as popular as vampires, but not far behind, zombies are all the rage on the small screen these days, and on the silver screen, too. Zombies even populate books, including a recent "survival guide" to an apocalyptic zombie invasion. What I can't find, however, is any mention of the fact that, science-fiction aside, we all have a bit of the zombie in us right here, right now, in real life.

Can't find it within you? The first place to look is your diet. Zombies, remember, began their lives as thinking, feeling, aware, and spiritually conscious human beings. Some imaginary agent erased these qualities—options that include a bite, a virus, a chemical, or an alien influence—leaving the zombie an unthinking, unfeeling, unaware, spiritually unconscious entity. In fictional settings, zombies devour whatever is available and whatever stands in their way. Freshly undead, they eat the flesh of the still living or the recently deceased. If it's available for consumption, zombies are interested. They have no sense whatsoever of any kind of natural balance, no sense of vanishing resources, and no sense of whether other zombies are getting enough to eat. If it's there, they go for it.

Zombies do not care if their food is processed. They do not care if their food has been genetically modified or cloned. They do not care if what they put into their mouths is rife with antibiotics, steroids, or chemicals vouchsafed by agribusiness, manufacturers, or an agency of questionable independence driven by questionable motives. They do not care if the food they eat is based on the liquid secretion of another species and intended for that other species' babies. Zombies cannot read all the scientific studies linking many of these ingredients with chronic, sometimes fatal diseases, nor, of course, can they excuse their unconscious behavior by claiming to have been influenced by powerful corporations running obfuscating spin ads with gigantic media budgets. Zombies don't know the straight scoop from a snow job; they don't even read.

Zombies don't mind eating themselves into a stupor—they're already in one. Zombies don't care if what they put in their mouth is loaded with minerals they don't need whilst lacking the ones they do. They particularly don't care if many of their foods are artificially and unnaturally flavored. They don't know or care if their food is polluted with too much salt or poisoned by the addition of a white powder derived from a tropical plant that was at one time treated by a drug by European nobility and thence only consumed in tiny quantities for titillation. Nope, zombies don't care about any of this, because being unthinking, unfeeling, and unaware, they lack the capacities of discipline, restraint, and quality of judgment. A zombie doesn't understand the concept of cause and effect and pays no heed to consequences. Put a zombie down in front of a holiday buffet, or office party snacks and booze, and just watch what happens.

Of course, zombie weirdness is not only about food, it's also about movement and exercise. Unlike their human precursors, Zombies are not built to move. Zombies will sit and gaze vacantly into space until prey comes along or until they smell something to eat. When a zombie does get up and move, it pays not the slightest attention to the quality, purpose, or results of their movements. It's not about healthful exercise or pleasure in using their body; it's just about a mindless putting of one foot in front of another. Zombies are not aware that movement without intention or purpose doesn't help their health; they aren't interested in health. They don't care about living and dying; they're already undead. Like sheep, they often move together as a unit, doing or avoiding precisely what other zombies do and avoid. Of course, zombies are not nearly as smart as sheep.

The zombie does have a nervous system, albeit a rudimentary one, so it may well wallow in the discomfort of an overstuffed belly and the pain of lower back muscles seldom or improperly used. It will not notice its own softness of mind, of course, since it doesn't even know it has a mind. The zombie is not aware of the perils of sitting for long periods at a desk or on a couch. Mindlessly watching television or stuffing cheesy snacks into its mouth are not habits a zombie avoids. If the snack is there, a zombie will eat it. If the TV is on, the zombie will watch it, regardless of programming quality or content.

If it even bothers to think that much, a zombie will assume that the frenzied ocean of materialism in which it swims is the only ocean there is, and that everyone else enjoys the water of conspicuous consumption just as much as it does. It has no room for the concept that Earth's resources are finite, that mining for fossil fuels is cracking Earth's crust, and that air and water quality matter to all sentient beings. It doesn't know what a sentient being is, because it is not one. Indeed, it has no need for deeper caring, no time for inner reflection, and no inclination to be compassionate towards others or to seek a meaningful connection with anyone. The zombie is all about the zombie.

Because the zombie accepts anything it hears or sees as fact—especially as it has been so trained by official agencies or the general flow of culture—it will not notice the gradual erosion of truth in media. It will not notice the steady increase in invasive technologies and the concurrent diminution of privacy. It will pay no attention to the insidious coupling of industry and government and the steady blurring of the line between corporate and governmental affairs. It will only notice the loss of those rights it has always taken for granted when someone shoots it with a flamethrower.

Most of all, the zombie does not notice the erosion of constitutional checks and balances, the growing disharmony between governors and governed, and the rising tide of totalitarianism. It accepts the carnivorous nature of rulers just as it accepts its own indiscriminate and unthinking appetite. It no more thinks to criticize acts of war and expansion of empire than to curb its own habit of stepping on the heads of dogs and sucking down the brains of hapless humans. It accepts the downward spiral of culture and civilization the same way it accepts the great mass extinction underway—which is to say, with unreserved disinterest.

It is the purpose of this manifesto to rid the world of zombies. I am, for the purposes of this colorful metaphor, the zombie-hunting monk and I am looking for lieutenants, corporals, privates and generals in my Mad Monk Militia.

CHAPTER FIVE

SENSITIVITY
AND ENVIRONMENT

I am privileged to belong to two distinct Daoist traditions. The one I have been affiliated with the longest is known as *Shangqing Dao*, the Way of Highest Clarity. This is the lineage of my long-term martial arts master, and extends all the way back to the first century of the Common Era. It places great emphasis on personal cultivation exercises, meditation, and the wisdom of canonical texts, some of which are medical in nature. It cleaves closely to Laozi and Zhuangzi's original prescriptions for the life of a sage. It is also rebellious by design, having been conceived partly in response to the social strictures of Confucianism. The second tradition, the one in which I was ordained a monk, is the *Longmen* lineage of the *Quanzhen Dao*, the Way of Complete Truth. Founded approximately a thousand years later, this tradition is more modern and social in nature and is characterized by a more well-developed organization. It incorporates elements of Confucian thought (in a fashion the previous tradition might have considered sacrilegious) and Buddhist ideas.

Both lineages put an emphasis on nature and environment, but in different ways. Ge Hong (283–343 CE), a key figure in early Daoist thinking and an influential teacher affiliated with the *Shangqing Dao* tradition, was perhaps most interested in nature as the source of sustenance and a fount of longevity. In his canonical text *Baopuzi Neipian*, "The Master Who Embraces Simplicity," he tells the story of some Han Dynasty hunters who spied what appeared to be a magical person covering the Zhongnan Mountain landscape (an important site in Daoist lore) with such ease and speed he appeared to be flying. The hunters pursued their prey for a long time before finding his lair and surprising him there. When they finally captured him, they discovered he was a she.

She told them she was more than two hundred years old, had been a member of a previous emperor's harem, and had fled into the woods when her dynasty fell. She had nearly starved to death in the wild but had been rescued by a forest hermit who showed her edible nuts, roots, and plants. She survived on these and became clear of mind, strong of body, and capable of amazing feats. Forced back into a diet of grains and meat while in the care of the hunters, however, she quickly aged and died, never reaching the transcendent state of which she had been capable. Ge Hong's point, of course, was that we eat too much and poorly and that there is salvation in the right natural diet.

Ge Hong was not only interested in nuts, roots, and magical mushrooms. He was also a big fan of the healing power of special, natural places. More to the point, though, he advocated for the cultivation of the numinous, nature-transcending qualities of human beings. He believed in activating those qualities by cleaving to a natural life and pursuing esoteric arts. In one way or another, all these arts were inspired by natural law. They emphasized the natural flow and cycles of the *qi* (energy) inside our bodies. *Shangqing* texts other than those written by Ge Hong describe alchemy (the goal being longevity and the growth of the spirit, not turning lead into gold) with such imagination and color that they shame the work of the greatest medieval European wizards. In these texts, areas in the body are deified (that is to say visualized as gods) and brought into congruence according to a cosmic order divined through meditation and disciplined observation of natural phenomena.

My other lineage, the more modern and expansive *Quanzhen Dao*, has blossomed in modern times, giving rise to a number of popular schools, institutions, and teaching communities. Many of these incorporate an appreciation for and understanding of nature into their daily practices, embracing tai chi, qigong health exercises, and *feng shui*—the art of arranging homes, buildings, living spaces, and objects for maximal health, fecundity, and prosperity. Despite the disdain for the trend in some orthodox religious and academic Daoist circles, this is the branch of Daoism most closely aligned with worldwide conservation and environmental movements. It is in the contemporary manifestations of this tradition that we can find an emphasis on sensitivity to the plight of nature and all sentient beings.

Sensitivity is required by all Daoist practices. We cannot excel in Daoist martial arts without being sensitive to the movements and intentions of opponents. We cannot create living spaces (never mind a life) without an awareness of natural forces and we cannot engage in Daoist sex practices without sensitivity to the feelings and energies of our partner. In the end, it will not be some intervening alien race or divine being who saves us and our planet from irreversible disaster. Rather, it will be recognizing ourselves to be made of the same stuff as our mountains, deserts, jungles, forests, and plains. Salvation will come when we realize we have been calved from the ground beneath our feet just as surely as ice is from water. It will be our sensitivity, manifested as love for Mother Earth, that will herald a new era of environmental restoration and rebirth.

· · ·

In my earliest years as a student of Daoism, with Laozi's ideas roiling around between my ears, I noticed how well the Daoist view of the world meshed with both the New Physics (which was just then creeping into the popular imagination) and Darwin's idea of natural selection through evolution. Daoism's natural core implied that the answers to life's deepest questions were to be found in the wild. Yearning for more exposure to nature, I applied for and won an Explorers Club Field Opportunity award, ending up in a vast, remote, and inhospitable Paraguayan jungle known as the Chaco Boreal.

I wasn't much of an outdoorsman or field biologist, but immediately found in that vast landscape the deep spiritual awareness Laozi extolled. Physical discomfort invigorated me. I relished feeling hungry and cold, waking up in blazing heat, covered in dust. I loved going to sleep with a crisp wind howling around me. The angry patter of hard rain on the sloping sides of my tent soothed me. I was terrified but also empowered when I had to fend off wolves with a burning stick, alone at night beneath a sky glittering with stars from horizon to horizon. I was thrilled to encounter an anteater on a jungle path and to have it follow me like a dog, then horrified when my expedition leader directed me to shoot it dead. I was terrified to hear a jaguar roar at me from a grassy hillock while I hunted frogs by their call.

Later, at Yale University, I sensed a thick curtain blocking my view of the deepest nature of things. While my classmates enthusiastically embraced the idea that rational inquiry would reveal the world, I wasn't so sure. Trying to memorize facts and figures, I longed to use my mind to connect with the universe, not to attack it with a pickaxe. I pined for the smoky, sensual aroma of green Palo Santo wood, the sounds of armadillos in the underbrush, the telltale rattle of vipers, and the thumping of bird wings. I noticed how my mood was tied to light and season. I felt bereft by the bare trees of winter, elated by the first rustlings of spring, soothed by summer thunder, and melancholic at the smell of burning timber and the sight of autumn leaves. Unable to sit still and focus the way others could, I was disheartened by the cynical reality of people going into medicine for money rather than healing, into law for the corner office rather than the fight against injustice, and into the arts for glory rather than the pure joy of self-expression.

After more years of school, a lengthy series of hard knocks, and more late-night reading about the lessons of nature, I returned to South America and hired a single-engine plane to fly me into the Chaco. At altitude, I saw nothing but thousands of square miles of utter devastation. Gone were the beautiful trees that had once beguiled me with their sweet, smoky aroma. Gone were the palms, lakes, ponds, and grasses. Gone were the birds, anteaters, tortoises, snakes, jaguars, and wild pigs. From horizon to horizon, nothing grew higher than my knee. Cattle for fast-food chains had trampled an entire jungle's vastness underfoot, all so Americans could eat cheap hamburgers.

To say I wept would be to understate the case. I felt as if I'd been kicked in the belly. I couldn't breathe. It was a moment I shall never, ever forget. Everything I'd sensed, felt, studied, and learned came together. I saw what human beings have become—what we've done to our world, the home we share with countless sentient beings. I understood the tragedy the human race is to Planet Earth and to each other. I understood this in human terms, in spiritual terms, in scientific terms, and, most clearly, in Daoist terms. I saw a species run amok, confused, angry, and destructive. I saw the beautiful balance of Planet Earth destroyed, and I have continued to see that horror unfolding every day and in every way, both in my frequent international travels and right here at home. There are few events in my life that more powerfully motivated me to be active in the world.

MANAGING RESOURCES

If there is a government function more important than protecting the environment, it has not yet been invented or conceived. Not only should any agency or branch charged with this mandate be given far-ranging powers, it must be staffed so fully that its agents can relentlessly and unceasingly run violators to ground. The problem, we must realize, is that saving the natural world doesn't look the way we want it to look. There is no way to remove human influence from the planet anymore. Despite the best efforts of conservationists who believe in buying up land to keep wild creatures safe from people, such protection is not ultimately feasible. Though many of us would rather it were otherwise, real conservation these days looks more like rescue workers scrubbing the oil off birds or kindly rangers gently diverting wolves. We have no greater priority than making sure we have a habitable planet for our children, grandchildren, great-grandchildren, and all other organisms.

· · ·

A keen aversion to waste is the first step towards conservation. Waste is a type of passive violence: passive because it is a side effect of sloth, inertia, habit, or disinterest; violent because it deprives those less fortunate (including sentient beings who cannot speak for themselves) of the resources they so often need. Waste takes so many forms that an entire book could be written on the subject. There is waste of personal energy (a finite quantity), oil, electricity, water, natural gas, and, of course, money. Being sensitive to wasteful behavior is a cornerstone of Daoism, as frugality is one of our Three Treasures. The Daoist concept of an effective, efficient life entails being careful with resources as well. Whether it is using elbow grease instead of a dishwasher, squeezing the last smidge out of a tube of toothpaste, riding a bike instead of driving a car, saving food (or purchasing less) rather than throwing it away, recycling clothes or resoling shoes instead of buying more, the list goes on and on. Why not take the time to critically examine our patterns of spending and use

and see where we could be more conservative? Planet Earth
will thank us.

. . .

We are in the middle of the Sixth Great Extinction in geologic
history. The unbridled growth of the human population and
our pernicious attitude towards our resources is the cause.
The systems on the planet can bear only limited loads, and
our resources are evaporating. There is a big difference
between lifting a great swath of humanity out of poverty and
providing them with the boundless luxuries of the Developed
World. The mere notion of a First, Second, or Third World
can no longer stand. There is only one world, one Earth, and
it cannot provide for our self-indulgent consumer lifestyle
any longer. We must come to see Earth as a macro-organism
that needs to be nourished, loved, and protected, rather than
as an inanimate, soulless ball of minerals meant to be chipped
at, drilled into, and blasted away until nothing is left. It is high
time we address the deep and keening emotional/spiritual
hole that has us constantly destroying our world and turning
what is beneath us into things we eventually discard. Material
overabundance has never provided anyone with lasting
happiness; it has, however, spelled out a death sentence for the
full, diverse, flowering, and beautiful version of Planet Earth
with which we are familiar.

. . .

Can we exalt sustainability and shun any appetite or activity
that diminishes finite levels of a natural resource? Replantation,
replenishment, and restoration are the enterprises of the
future. If we make the right moves, sustainable engineering
will soon become a hot new field of enterprise. To repair the

damage we have caused during the course of modern history, we must focus our time and attention on the workings of the world while lovingly following the natural cues that are available to us.

. . .

Preserving dirty industries such as coal mining and oil drilling is often excused in the name of lifestyle and employment. Defenders and proponents of these antiquated and earth-hating technologies claim it's unfair to deprive people of their traditional livelihood. Would we say the same if their business was murdering children today, rather than killing our progeny by raping the environment until it will no longer sustain them? Skills transfer. We can move workers from unsustainable energy industries to solar, wind, hydro, wave, and other emerging energy fields. We can give these folks jobs in water management, where they can rehabilitate and protect wetlands and coastlines. We can provide them jobs running tidal generators and building and maintaining wind farms. We can employ them to construct and run a solar grid in the Southwestern desert, which would be big enough to provide electricity to everyone in America, no muss, no fuss, no coal, no smog. We have to think big and we have to move forward, for everyone's sake.

. . .

The energetic cost of maintaining perfectly comfortable indoor temperatures is astonishingly high. This is especially true in hotels, airports, and other public venues. Rather than turning up the heat, why not put on a sweater? Rather than turning up the air conditioning, why not take that sweater off? Insisting we be perfectly comfortable at all times, even if that means stripping even more fossil fuels out of the ground or damming yet another river to make the electricity "we need," is self-indulgent in the extreme. Let's not only advocate for the sane use of power and temperature control in public spaces, but also cultivate energy-saving personal habits. Let's exercise discretion with our home thermostat, closing windows and doors when the air conditioning is on. Let's leave blinds drawn against the sun. Reducing our dependence upon planet-killing fuels is easy, yet we still don't do it. Let's show consideration to our home planet by being miserly with our resources.

. . .

The continued use of fossil fuels will turn us all into fossils, particularly as our populations swell. It is high time to stop plundering non-renewable resources by fracking and strip mining. It is also best to avoid nuclear power, despite its low short-term costs, because of its potential to wreak extreme destruction on the planet. While we advocate for carbon emission reduction, let's explore wave, solar, and geothermal energy sources. Let's develop tidal generators, algal biofuels, and cold fusion for a clean future. Let us reject any narrative claiming natural gas to be a desirable energy source. Natural gas is methane, a damaging environmental pollutant. Extracting it destroys wilderness areas and sullies ground water and is, in fact, no cleaner to burn than coal when compared against the latest generation of clean-burning plants. Natural gas is, at best, a stopgap measure and, at worst, a distraction from research into truly clean, renewable, and sustainable energy. It is high time to clear out the deadwood of oil-company interests and strip their agendas from the energy sector. The greedy influence of industrial special interests has no place in resource management and energy policy. Using new and higher taxes on fossil fuels to provide capital for the development of sustainable, clean alternatives is the formula we need to transform our relationship with energy.

• • •

Although the most appealing trains are still those that meander slowly through a beautiful landscape, the bullet trains of Europe and Asia are fabulously efficient people-movers that must rise to the forefront of the transportation industry worldwide. They are sleek, powerful, and impressive, and it is truly technologically marvelous to move large numbers of commuters and travelers so safely, comfortably, quickly, and efficiently. Despite the fun, freedom, and convenience it offers, the personal automobile is a dinosaur. Time to wean ourselves from our love affair with the automobile and embrace the efficient, environmentally-friendly, and socially inclusive railcar. As we go through that process, let's begin by turning away from trucks and other heavy vehicles as personal transportation, limit cars to no more than a ton, and outlaw recreational vehicles in pristine natural areas. After all, what kind of fun, and for what kind of person, is worth destroying the natural habitats of sentient beings for our own transient gratification?

• • •

For pity's sake, let's turn off our engines when we're stuck in traffic. Let's be conscious enough of our own consumption to recognize when we're pumping heat and greenhouse gases into the atmosphere for absolutely no reason at all. Trucks spewing diesel fumes into the air as they idle near loading docks, ports, or border crossings are simply symbols of the very kind of unconsciousness it is incumbent upon all of us to shake awake.

...

When speaking of *nature* and what is natural, let us be cautious. We no longer know the meaning of that word the way we did in aboriginal times, when our senses were attuned to shifts and changes and cues. Any sense of "nature" now is tainted by an addiction to bending it to our will as we do in creating city, regional, and national parks. To refer to nature in both spiritual and scientific terms is to reference a state of harmony and balance that exists only in theory and only in the past. Few of us will ever get a chance to see, feel, taste, hear, or smell a pristine natural environment. If this tragic fact does not provide motivation to save what is left, what will?

THE ILLUSION OF SEPARATION

Some time ago, when I still had quite a menagerie, a friend asked me why I bothered keeping amphibians and reptiles. I was surprised by the question, given that this friend was a great and compassionate animal lover who lived in a house full of dogs and cats and devoted himself endlessly to their pleasure. It took me a moment or two to formulate an answer.

"I take care of them," I said.

"Yes, but do they take care of you back? Do they even know you? I mean, a dog obviously does, and a cat too, at least if it's her fancy, but salamanders aren't exactly warm and fuzzy."

In my case, that's a good thing, because I'm allergic to most animals with hair—I'm even allergic to certain people—although, at times, I torture my immune system by keeping them around. I started to defend the intrinsic value of herps (the nickname of reptiles and amphibians, based on the Greek word for crawling) but stopped myself.

"It doesn't matter if you're taking care of a python or a koala bear," I said. "I get a charge out of the caretaking itself. It's a form of compassion to make sure that a creature who depends upon you has a good life. It's pure love, you know, the emotion that all those medical studies show does us good deep down in the neurotransmitter department."

"But who cares about the caretaking if the animal doesn't know you?"

"My animals certainly know me," I said. "But even if they didn't, altruistic behavior is good for the altruist. It drops blood pressure, lowers cholesterol, and boosts the immune system. I nurture those pets in my backyard and spare room for the same reason people grow plants in a greenhouse or on their kitchen windowsill, the same reason all kids want to be zookeepers; I do it because it feels good."

"Really?" he said. "I've seen snake poop and it's not pretty."

"My backyard is a Daoist garden," I said. "Poop is picked up and recycled, the soil is enriched by it, and my gardenias and jasmine plants flower and grow."

He paused, apparently looking for a new tactic. "If you're such an animal lover, how can you feed crickets and worms to your amphibians and mice and rats to your lizards and snakes?"

"Feeding my pets is part of the responsibility of owning them. The rodents I feed them are bred in captivity specifically for the purpose of feeding reptiles. The reptiles and amphibians I keep are also bred in captivity. It's a closed system that mimics nature without disturbing

the greater world directly. No animal I keep was ever free in the wild, not the pets themselves, and not the food they eat."

"There is suffering in dying in a snake's jaws," he pursued. "I thought you were all about reducing suffering. You won't eat animals yourself!"

"I can survive and even thrive on a vegan diet," I said. "Snakes and most lizards cannot."

"I suppose you're going to tell me that feeding a rat to a snake is meditation."

"It's a reminder of the cycle of life. Remember, meditation is at least in part about expanding your perceptions and connecting with something greater than you. That realization is a comfort and a deepening of the experience of living. It also generates compassion. I find satisfaction in creating a natural environment in which living creatures can thrive."

"Why not get a parrot? At least one of those can talk back to you."

"I paid for a lot of graduate school buying sick and abandoned parrots, nursing them back to health, and selling them to stable, loving homes. I grew quite sensitive to feather dust in the process and my lungs can no longer tolerate birds in the house. Anyway, I've just finished explaining that the particular type of animal is beside the point."

"Yet you have a soft spot for reptiles," he interrupted, treating the conversation as an argument and sensing victory for his point.

"Preferences," I said. "I know a monk is not supposed to have them but I'm not quite at the stage where I've abandoned all of mine. I admire the quiet stoicism, longevity, diversity, and staying power of reptiles. I

love to think about how long they've been on the planet. Doesn't hurt that they don't make me sneeze, either."

"I surrender," he said, bringing the conversation to a close.

As local, limited, and self-serving as my pet care may seem, I would like to think that the example pet care sets, particularly for children, may help nudge attitudes about the living world away from their downward global spiral of cruelty, narcissism, and destruction, and towards a healthier, and more sustainable and compassionate direction. Imagine, just for a moment, what the world would look like if we all set aside our games and diversions for a while and cared for the world's frogs and the polar bears and the tarantulas and the squid—fed them, protected their homes, showed our consciousness by our actions. What a world we would have if we turned off the TV in favor of the sounds of birds and noticed, with a growing sense of profound unease, that they are gradually fading away.

Awareness of the presence, pain, pleasure, and rights of non-human sentient beings is the next step in our spiritual evolution. It is critical to financially, politically, and practically bolster dedicated hobbyists and zoos in their efforts to propagate endangered species of all kinds, from plants to elephants. In this we can keep vanishing genomes alive until such time as we can reintroduce them to a stabilized world. In the same way that forward-thinking botanists have created seed banks around the world, and in the same cooperative spirit as so many have donated personal computer time to SETI (the Search for Extra-Terrestrial Intelligence), why not dedicate some space in our own homes to the preservation of the glorious diversity of plant and animal life while we struggle on other fronts to save the planet to which they belong?

. . .

Getting in touch with nature after a lifetime of disconnection requires only a change of habit. The appreciation and deep-down knowing are there. Don't think so? How about a sunset? That's nature. Even if we watch it from the window of an apartment deep in a ghetto rife with drugs and violence, the sun and moon still shine through. The fastest and most accessible route to contact with nature is to have a dog, a cat, a bird, a snake, or even an aquarium fish. If none of those work, there are always plants. Even people who work long hours and travel frequently can manage a garden, though it may be as small as a terrarium in the kitchen. The size or exoticness of our garden is not the thing; neither are the bounteous colors or the luscious vegetables. The thing is the caregiving, the nurturing, the watching, the noticing when things are too wet or too dry, the observation of when plants are getting too much sun or not enough, the meditating while watering. Let's do the watering ourselves instead of leaving it to automatic systems. Giving water is giving life. Talk about cheap therapy. Talk about cultivating sensitivity. Talk about re-engaging with the world around us. Let's slow down and reap all the benefits of watering our gardens by hand. Let's press our fingers into the dirt, touch and play music for our plants (yes, they respond to it), and grow our souls in the process.

. . .

All living things on Earth share the same genetic material, the same code, and the same information. They all have some degree of awareness, and some version of feelings and thoughts. *Qi* runs through all living things as a hand moves the fingers of a glove. This force is the same whether we call the gloves people, cherry trees, cockroaches, or eels. Culling wolves, coyotes, and other sentient beings by using steel-jaw traps and cyanide bombs is a sign that we haven't yet realized that no species is more entitled to survive than any other. Wherefrom did the strange and distant cruelty, rife with the cold, cold hygiene of distance, lead us to set such devices and then walk away, knowing full well the long-lasting terror and agony that must ensue? Isn't it time we found compassion for all living creatures, including our fellow humans? Isn't it time we woke up to the reality of the common thread that ties the natural world together rather than indulging in the fantasy that we are any better, or even fundamentally different, from anyone or anything else which lives and breathes on Planet Earth?

. . .

The search for extra-terrestrial intelligence gets more airplay and is somehow deemed more romantic than appreciating, understanding, and communicating with octopi, squid, and corvid birds like ravens and crows, who have developed great intelligence by following a different evolutionary path than our own. How strange! These species share our world and are venerated by some aboriginal societies, yet we devour or poison them rather than learning to communicate with them and finding out what they know of our world. And then there are the whales, which we harpoon, butcher, and torture to suicide with naval sonar while evidence continues to mount that their worldview and mental achievements may be broader and greater than our own. Such crimes cause great suffering and demean us daily. Firing at birds with shotguns to avoid losing a few kernels of corn, frying the brains of cetaceans in the interests of our petty, national squabbles—this all must stop. What could be more important than preserving intelligent life right here on this beautiful blue planet and coming to a better understanding of it, too?

...

Plants and animals live in accordance with their natures
and thus know exactly what they are doing. How is it that
we have so thoroughly and completely lost our way? Is it a
consequence of having developed agriculture and forgotten
how to read our environment for cues to our own sustenance?
Is it a consequence of having multiplied to the point that our
natural niche has disappeared? If we are to wander through
gardens and castles of the mind, why not build them in concert
with nature? When seeking our mission, our purpose, and
our place in life, why not consider the vast workings of the
universe instead of our own transient urges? Why not quest
more deeply for life's meaning and ask ourselves where we are
needed and how we can help? Let us discover that we were
meant not to be competitors and destroyers, but nurturers of
each other and stewards of our world.

...

*As a child paddling a canoe on a river in Connecticut, I saw an
Eastern Painted Turtle basking on a log. Impulsively, I reached for
it with my paddle and flipped it into the boat. It scrambled around
madly, its little claws making a ruckus against the aluminum hull, its
eyes bright in its yellow-striped head, its moss-covered, red-rimmed
shell a mystery. I put it back in the water but held onto it, wondering
for a moment whether all the frantic energy in those little webbed feet
might actually be enough to pull my canoe along. Feeling its energy, I
brought it back into the boat.*

*I took it home with me that day. I set up a little plastic home for it,
the kind with a ramp and a green plastic palm tree. I fed it fish pellets
and hamburger and crickets and worms. After a time, it stopped
diving into the water at the sight of me, watched me while I did my*

homework, moved around when I played music, and went to sleep when I did. To everyone's surprise, except maybe my own, it thrived, eating like a champ—even, eventually, from my fingers. When it grew, I set up an aquarium for it, replete with a pump, filter, and lights designed to stand in for the sun in the indoor darkness of my parents' New York City apartment.

A lifelong love affair between me and the turtles of the world began with that charming creature. I took to my new passion with gusto, reading everything I could about turtles, watching every TV special about them, and begging my parents to take me to zoos and aquaria wherever the family traveled, in hopes of a glimpse of one of the exotic species I'd read about.

There are only a few hundred species of turtles in the world. I learned the Latin names of most of them and became familiar with their natural history, too. When I discovered that a pet emporium on Third Avenue actually sold some of those exotics, the flickering candle of my interest roared into a house fire of obsession. I did odd jobs, hoarded my nickels and dimes, and saved up enough money to actually buy some of the exotics I'd been reading about. Over the next couple of years, I bought quite a few turtles, including a mud turtle from Mexico, a helmeted terrapin from Africa, an Arrau River turtle from British Guiana, a yellow-spotted river turtle from the Amazon, a diamondback terrapin from the North Carolina coast, a little Reeve's turtle from Japan, and a lovely flap-shelled turtle, a species that used to range all over the Indian subcontinent but has become a widely exploited and highly endangered species.

Initially, I had all these animals in small aquariums. My bedroom looked more like the reptile house at the Bronx Zoo—which I frequently visited and where I would later intern—than like the abode of a city kid. After a time, however, I came to realize just how alert and aware my turtles were and how bored and lonely they must be living isolated and alone. I could not afford one of the oversized tanks used by zoos, but I could manage a plastic wading pool of the sort suburban children use for summertime splashing. I put a pond filter in it, constructed an island on which the turtles could climb out and, voila, my pets had more than a hundred gallons in which to cavort.

Even as a child, I had mixed feelings about taking animals out of the wild simply for my own gratification. Once, I even had a dream about how badly my little painted turtle wanted to be back in his river, circumnavigating the duckweed, frolicking in the current, free to find his own food and choose his own friends, hiding places, and basking spots. All the same, it was marvelously satisfying to create a miniature world for my pets, and I took pride and pleasure in seeing them thrive.

One afternoon, wandering the streets of New York City's Chinatown, I came across a fish vendor offering for sale several species of softshell turtles and a chicken turtle, a species from North America. Dumped in a dry bucket and out on the cold street without needed heat, their shells were cracked and dinged, and some bled from sores on the legs and neck. A customer saw me looking at them and told me the softshell varieties were a better choice because they were easier to cook. I watched in horror as the vendor decapitated one of those right then and there, dumping the body into a plastic bag. The severed head fell, eyes wide in disbelief, jaws working to bite the sawdust on the sidewalk, alive for what seemed like hours but was probably just a few minutes.

At that time, I didn't know that turtles had an historic role in traditional Chinese medicine, allegedly providing cures for everything from impotence to cancer. I had no idea that nearly half a century later, consequent to myths, appetites, and environmental devastation, China would be the epicenter of a shelled-reptile genocide. I couldn't rescue every turtle in Chinatown that day but I knew the chicken turtle would have a good life with the other eight turtles in my wading pool, so I bought him and took him home.

He did not have a good life at all; in fact he was dead the very next morning. Upon examination, I saw he had a bite in his neck. I'd never seen turtles act violently toward each other and figured he must have been injured at the market stall. It was the first time I'd lost a pet and I was devastated. I took the subway to Chinatown a couple of days later and rescued another one. The next morning, my Indian flapshell turtle was dead. I couldn't believe it. That animal, my favorite, had been thriving. He too had a gash on his neck. Not thinking terribly clearly about the problem, I replaced him with a different exotic, a snake-neck turtle from Australia. The next morning, that Arrau River turtle was dead.

And so it went for the next couple of weeks. It gradually dawned on me that so long as there were nine turtles in the pool, everything was fine. Add a tenth one, though, and the next morning I'd find one dead, bitten in the neck. By process of attrition and, finally, observation, I discovered the diamondback terrapin to be the culprit. So long as the pool was not too crowded, his aggressive tendencies lay dormant. Up the population density by a single turtle, however, and he went on a murderous rampage.

I talked to my school biology teacher about it, and he explained the concept of carrying capacity. An environment can only handle so much, he explained. Tax it further, deplete its resources (including space), and nature will balance things out. I was not yet completely Daoist, but I realized that the diamondback was not a murderer but an instrument of Dao, of natural forces. It was doing what needed to be done to maintain balance in the environment in which it lived. I gave it to a friend who lived in North Carolina. He set it free in a brackish marsh on the edge of the ocean, right where the species is most comfortable. In the spring, I took the painted turtle back to the same Connecticut river in which I'd caught it and had a little ceremony, alone in my canoe under the sun, as I watched it swim away. I kept the other turtles for years.

To the time of this writing, every day in my life begins and ends with caring for turtles, waking them up in the morning with fresh food and clean water and helping them settle in for the night in an outdoor pen or pool, safe from predators. Can't say why I still do it, as the rest of humanity seems bent on their extermination, nor can I say why I still love them. It's just the way it is.

• • •

Some people find in pets an opportunity to love and be loved in a way that has not otherwise happened for them. Domesticated species are best if such companionship is our goal, although certain other species such as ferrets and parrots can also develop relationships with us. The question of keeping exotic animals is a bit more complex. On the one hand, most of us are poorly equipped and inadequately trained to provide what such animals need to thrive. More, the trade in exotic animals continues to decimate native populations and often wreaks havoc upon the environment. If we *do* decide to keep exotic animals, let's eschew wild-caught animals and buy instead from legitimate private breeders, folks who have dedicated their time and resources to really learning how to make exotics happy. Depleting nature of sentient beings for our own amusement is nearly as reprehensible as euthanizing pets because they are no longer convenient or easy to care for. If we can no longer care for a pet, domestic or exotic, we are obliged to find someone who can. Why not support no-kill shelters and rehabilitation centers?

• • •

Our fetish for domestic felines has created a pernicious imbalance in the world. Cute and cuddly as some housecats may seem while still kittens, those that have escaped the confines of human habitation and become feral ravage ecosystems by preying on billions of native creatures such as songbirds every year. Sad as it may seem, feral cats must be trapped and placed in secure homes. Failing this, they must be humanely euthanized to stem the dire and global ecological imbalances their presence create. Dogs, by contrast, are truly wired to be contributing members of our families. Not only do they work for us on ranches and farms, they provide companionship, succor, and protection, and have thus truly evolved to be our best friends. Responsible dog ownership, however, means preventing accidental coupling to avoid overpopulation. This means keeping control of our dogs, keeping them inside, and disallowing unplanned couplings. It does not mean "fixing" our pets. Outside of extreme circumstances, and perhaps even then, sterilization of sentient creatures is mutilation and cannot be condoned by civilized society.

...

The literally shameful day of zoos and aquaria as entertainment venues is over. Such parks have new and more important purposes now. First and foremost, zoos must run captive breeding and DNA preservation programs for those species that human animals have brought to, and across, the line of extinction. Second, they must inspire in all of us a love and respect for other sentient beings, and educate children about their responsibility to preserve the natural world for the future. Let's vote with our wallets by boycotting all institutions that have not made the above priorities transparent and evident.

OUR BLUE PLANET

The channel between the coast of Santa Barbara, California, and the string of islands just offshore is a marine sanctuary in more ways than one. A so-called transition zone, it is one of the most biologically rich and active areas on Earth. Scores of endangered species seek refuge in its oxygen-rich water, benefiting from the upwelling of nutrients that comes when the warm southern currents meet the cold northern ones. The blue whale is the most magnificent of these. The largest animal to have ever graced the planet (and yes, that includes the dinosaurs), it can reach nearly a hundred feet and weight more than 170 tons. Before modern, commercial whaling began, blue whales could be found in nearly all the world's oceans. Today, there are relatively few left alive.

Only once in the years that I lived beside it did word come that blue whales had made an appearance in the channel. A good friend owned a twenty-eight-foot fishing boat with a tuna tower. He offered to take me and my wife out into the channel to see if we could spot one of the legendary giants. When we arrived at the dock for an early departure, the air was cool enough to require a thick sweater; the horizon was visible as a yellow glow and a broad, gray blanket of fog hung over a perfectly calm sea. Powering steadily away from the coastline, seabirds, puffins, petrels, pelicans, guillemots, and cormorants numbering in the tens of thousands flitted in and out of view, sometimes coming to rest on the surface. Heads of kelp broke water like brown-haired children swimming. Several large blue sharks followed us for a while but were eventually replaced by a pod of small, white, flat-faced whales, impressive with their tall dorsal fins and leaping breaches. I learned later these were Risso's whales, which the Taiwanese call monkey dolphins.

As we approached the boundary of the channel, we saw a couple of commercial whale-watching vessels converging on a spot near Santa

Rosa Island, its dry cliffs brown and its shoreline austere. Figuring they had fish-finding equipment, we followed at a respectful distance, as much to avoid the noise from their packed decks as to avoid being tossed in their wakes. Abruptly, my friend turned the boat and headed in another direction.

"What's up?" I asked him.

His hands were on the wheel so he used his chin to gesture at an area of thin cloud cover, beneath it a shimmering patch where seabirds and sea lions gamboled with porpoises.

"That ray of light," he said. "It's like God's finger's pointing."

Soon, Pacific white-sided dolphins surrounded us, riding our bow wave and surfing back and forth across our path. We could hear the popping hiss of their breathing when they broke water. My wife lay down on the bow and reached out for them, screaming with pleasure as she touched their sleek, hard bodies.

"Their backs are scarred," she said sadly.

"Propellers," my friend opined. "Bane of dolphins and sea turtles far and wide."

As abruptly as it had appeared, the light from the sky was gone, squeezed out of existence by a clenching of clouds. The dolphins disappeared, and the sea birds flapped off. I felt lost in the new marine, quiet and empty, almost as if night had fallen on a day to remember.

We turned around and headed back toward the island. Unexpectedly, the surface of the sea opened up ahead. I thought for a moment we had encountered a submarine from the nearby Ventura County Naval Base, but then a mountain of broad, blue flesh appeared, rolled, and went under.

"Blue whale," my friend said matter-of-factly, throttling the
engine back.

We waited and it rose again, this time in the company of another. We
tried to draw closer but the whales moved off. A third appeared, and
the tour boat, which had been dogging us, veered toward it. Suddenly,
a whale spouted close by. The noise was explosive, startling, and the
fountain bigger than a fire hose's issue. A foul, fishy stench wafted
toward us.

"Let's just sit here a bit," said my friend, climbing up the tuna tower
for a better look at the water below.

I went to the stern and sat down less than two feet away from the
surface. Idly, I imagined how easily one of the giants could upend our
fragile bit of floating flotsam, motorized or not. I dipped my fingers
into the cold water as if to test how long I might last immersed in it.
A moment later, we started to move. The motion felt different, not
the predictable pitch and yaw of an insistent sea but something more
purposeful and alive. My friend switched off the engine and I looked
up at him inquiringly. He replied with a look of holy terror.

The whale was beneath us, his blue skin reflecting the sky and
turning the water white beneath our hull. My wife appeared
wordlessly at my side as he passed beneath the boat, close enough
for us to touch him had we dared. For some reason, I felt inclined to
count how long it took for him to pass below us, an urge to quantify
the experience in some way, perhaps sensing one day I would share
the story.

"One," I said. "Two. Three. Four. Five..."

I counted to seventeen before the trailing edge of his massive tail
cleared us. He moved away then, his bow wave showing his track,
then barrel-rolled to raise a fin taller than a ranch-style house. The

tourists off our bow whistled and clapped. The whale turned and
came for us again, and I leaned toward him this time, somehow
emboldened by what I sensed was his goodwill, my center of gravity
over the water, my grip on the gunwale all that was keeping me in the
boat. His head broke water not five feet from mine, his mouth a long
line pulled back as if in a smile.

It wasn't his size that did it to me, nor his pungent, alien fragrance.
It was, instead, his eye. Brimming with so much consciousness it
seemed as if it might explode. It was the size of a dinner plate, its
pupil jet black, socket roughly the dimensions of a family-size pizza.
The look it gave me was filled not only with knowledge I could never
share, but with a sense he knew of our connection, understood all
which we humans so often ignore, namely that we are all cut from
the same cloth and share the same home, the same thoughts, and the
same fate. He was curious enough about me to stay in that position
for a few long seconds, holding his body out of the water with
pumps of his powerful tail, and issuing me, above all, an expression
of compassion.

Compassion! Even after all we humans have done to his kind—the
bursting nuclear reactors, the lost and leaking vessels, the islands
of plastic, the poison of industrial effluents, the abuses of long-line
fishing and drift nets, the spilling of riverine sewage, and, of course,
the relentless, deliberate slaughter (using satellite surveillance and
explosive harpoons) for meat, blubber, and the oily essence, ambergris,
we use in perfume.

Am I anthropomorphizing? Am I attributing human characteristics
to a creature whose intelligence is, by any measure other than the
ability to manipulate objects with absent hands, at least the equal
of our own? I hope so. Rather than losing tenure for doing so, I wish
scientists would anthropomorphize too and, in that way, acknowledge
that all they can possibly know is, and will always be, framed by

human experience, interpreted by the human mind, and experienced through the human sensorium.

I cried. The whale, apparently satisfied, sank back beneath the surface. The tour boat sent a skiff our way and its passengers used glass-bottomed buckets to scan the ocean for the blue. I sat back down and stared at the water. In the distance, two more blue whales breached. A shark cruised by, ignoring me, even though I was heating the water not far from him with my tears.

• • •

Using the oceans as our toilet besmirches our already highly dubious reputation as a species, and is tantamount to soiling our own bed, something we only do when we are newly born or sick. There is no ocean-wide flushing lever, no float bowl or sewage pipe draining our magnificent seas. There is nowhere for our waste to go once we dump it there. Imagine what sentient beings swimming through our waste think of us. Imagine how you would like hiking through theirs. To add insult to injury, ocean acidification caused by the emission of carbon dioxide and other greenhouse gases may well be the greatest single threat to life on Earth. All life sprang from the deep blue sea, and all life still depends upon it for oxygen, sustenance, refuge, and rejuvenation. Our very future depends upon giving ocean restoration and preservation the highest possible priority.

• • •

If we enjoy fish for the lean protein, taste, and anti-inflammatory oils, we may be unaware of the problems of ocean bycatch. This is the polite and sanitized phrase for animals unintentionally killed in the process of commercial fishing, whose long lines and vast drift nets do not discriminate between the species fishermen are after and sea turtles, marine mammals, non-commercial fish species, and ocean rarities. Some estimates say roughly a quarter of the living creatures caught in nets are wasted, meaning they don't make it to store or table. The actual percentage may be much higher. Shrimp fishing is especially culpable. Imagine taking a pail to the seashore and scooping up a bucket of sand, seaweed, and water. Can we be sure we will only get one kind of seaweed? Sand grains of a particular color and shape? We cannot, and neither can commercial fisheries, whose practice is decimating wild populations among the splendid array of marine creatures. Fish farming is little better for, although it is less wasteful, it is just as cruel and results in more pollution. If our ocean ecosystems are to survive, the best answer is to put an end to our relentless war on the splendid array of marine creatures we wittingly and unwittingly kill, boycott all seafood products, and legislate commercial fishing out of existence.

. . .

We do not hunt cows for pleasure, yet tens of millions of us indulge in the unimaginably cruel activity known as recreational fishing. While more and more scientific studies show that fish feel pain, think creatively, engage in a multitude of different types of play, and bond with each other, we continue to torture them for sport, rip out their guts with hooks, rupture their innards, and, perhaps worst of all, dump them in bins where they slowly die gasping for air. The most important lesson we can learn from this activity—though not, of course, from the standpoint of the fish—is that we have an almost limitless ability to pretend we don't know something, to ignore the obvious suffering of sentient beings, from insects to our fellow humans, and to unthinkingly and uncaringly cause needless suffering. What say we start on the path to conscious living and a vegan diet by eliminating fishing for sport?

. . .

Our addiction to plastic is most assuredly the cause of environmental catastrophe, particularly in the marine environment. Islands made entirely of trash exist in the Pacific Gyre, plastic being their backbone. At last count, there were five trillion pieces of plastic polluting our oceans, amounting to 270,000 tons. This number will certainly be higher by the time you read this book. Sea turtles mistake plastic for jellyfish and choke to death on it. Whales and other sea creatures become entangled in it. Biodegradation, long considered acceptable, has proven to be toxic to the marine environment in ways we never imagined. Let's keep plastic out of the ocean, especially since some types have recently been shown to biodegrade over time. Why not limit our use of plastic in general? Despite industry efforts to obfuscate or hide study data—some of which links plastic to cancer—plastic use is increasingly proving harmful to humans as well as to oceans, leaching chemicals we don't really know much about into the water we drink and the food we eat. We are better off storing food in glass containers than in plastic bags, better off eating and drinking from metal and glass, better off using metal utensils. Of course, plastic not only hurts the ocean but creates toxic landfills and runoff on land as well. Let's develop substitutes for plastics as soon as possible. Right now, glass, which can be endlessly recycled, is a good choice. Let's not buy water in plastic bottles except in emergencies.

. . .

In terms of energetic efficiency and environmental impact, private aviation is an affront to a balanced world. Wherever did we get the idea that wealth gives us the right to selfishly consume fossil fuels, pollute with noise and fumes, and turn natural habitats into airports and runways? No individual is important enough to fly high over the masses caught in traffic below, simply to indulge his or her pleasure. Let's tap general aviation personnel to help us design better massive-people-movers, raise the performance of commercial aviation, and lower the cost of travel for everyday people. Private aircraft are symbols of wealth inequity and disregard for resources and, with the exception of their use for emergency relief and charitable work, must be shunned. Why not try hang gliders and windsurfing instead, to enjoy the ocean and the air while leaving the environment unmolested?

. . .

Apart from air and water, sand is the resource most used by human beings. This underappreciated resource is an essential element for building, and unbridled development in the Third World, particularly in Asia, has led to the large-scale rape of sand resources in a fashion largely unknown and unseen to non-locals. Erosion, air and water pollution, and devastation of marine ecosystems are the result, along with the destruction of towns, villages, and ways of life for countless voiceless populations in tropical locales far from First World eyes. Whole Indonesian islands have been removed from the global landscape, their underpinnings mechanically removed and shipped off to places like China, where they are used for concrete and foundations, often for projects that will never house a human soul. Real estate scams, speculations, money-laundering, political gambits, and more have made the sand wars breeding grounds for criminal gangs, corruption, murder, and environmental catastrophe. The more light we shed on such shenanigans, the more restraint we exercise in depleting our planet of its resources. Let's use this critical, non-renewable resource with greater care and circumspection.

$$\cdots$$

Powerboats are as deleterious to the seas as private aircraft are to the skies. Burning fossil fuels, they pollute our waterways to the point where many will no longer sustain life. The fuel, oil, and other effluents from race boats, ski boats, pleasure boats, and fishing vessels destroy coral reefs, wound and kill marine creatures ranging from nudibranchs and clams to reef fishes. Luxury yachts are not only a howling cry for the redistribution of wealth, but also a sign that money entitles some members of society to the most egregious possible levels of waste. Worst of all are cruise ships, which encourage unhealthy overeating and drinking—thereby perpetuating the devilish relationship between the food and healthcare industries—all the while spewing tons of raw sewage into the sea. Pleasure vessels on the sea should only be powered by paddle or sail. The intricacies and satisfaction of sailing, kayaking, and canoeing are joys not to be missed.

$$\cdots$$

One of the most frightening environmental catastrophes we face is the vanishing supply of fresh water. Overpopulation, the growth of non-sustainable industries, unconstrained development, water waste, and the desertification of the planet resulting from climate change, all combine to paint a frightening picture of a world. We will soon run out of enough potable water to sustain life as we know it. The inevitable result of this sort of shortage is so-called "water stress." Manifestations of such stress include the collapse of real estate and countless businesses to water wars and lethal droughts affecting untold millions. It is past time to hold our governments accountable for developing sustainable levels of water use by agriculture and industry, to legislate and enforce laws against pollution and waste, and to develop new guidelines for recycling and the protection of reservoirs and lakes. In addition, we will need new and radically more efficient desalination processes and plants. Let's develop better water use habits. Let's take shorter showers and fewer baths. Let's turn off the water when brushing our teeth or shaving. Let's forego laundering small loads and lower our expectations for luxury water use, such as fountains, gardens, and ornamental pools.

FINDING OUR ROOTS

Years ago, at a "cosmic" breakfast with famed author and Zen Grandmaster Peter Matthiessen, I posited that a cigarette butt I spied on the then-pristine Galapagos Island of Bartholomew was out of place and needed to be picked up. Matthiessen countered that the butt was exactly where it was supposed to be and that any perceived disturbance was within me rather than on the ground. While I understood this familiar Buddhist philosophical position, I argued then that I was also where I was supposed to be, and my impulse to do the right thing—pick up a piece of trash—was congruent with even the loftiest of philosophies. We proceeded to explore how unbridled personal convictions could lead to bad places—the Nazi Holocaust, for instance—but, despite my respect for Zen, I remain convinced that certain (not all) natural, biological impulses transcend intellection.

I thought about our discussion again a few years later when South Florida, my home at the time, endured a record-breaking cold spell. Needing a warm sun to survive, reptiles suffered most. Streets, backyards, driveways, outdoor malls, and walkways were suddenly littered with lizards and snakes, cold-sensitive, non-native species such as green iguanas and Cuban knight anoles which had arrived in shipments of bananas and other foodstuffs. The vast majority were dead, frozen solid by the combination of persistent low temperatures and high winds. Their slow, agonizing deaths broke my heart, but it was the survivors who needed help. It was a big task, for which I enlisted my ten-year-old son.

"I have a job for you," I said.

"Of course you do," he answered, no stranger to sarcasm even at his tender age.

"More important than finishing that Lego, as nice a toy as it may be."

"You think everything is more important than me having fun."

"How about compassion?" I said. "How about saving lives?"

This caught his attention, as I'd raised him to count compassion, along with kung fu, tea, love, books, and wild nature among the world's "great things." Reluctantly he got up, and we went out driving to rescue dying creatures. In the car, we listened to radio news of homeless people dying as the cold front spread west, and about sea turtles, caught in the cold weather, being found floating torpid on the sea.

"There's a lot of bad stuff going on right now," he said quietly.

"There is," I agreed. "But right here, right now, we get a chance to do some good."

As we drove around, we saw people with shovels and rakes trying to finish what the cold snap had started. Seeing the lizards treated not as sentient beings in need of compassionate aid but as pests ripe for killing, my boy screamed in horror and leapt out of the car almost before I could stop him. I backed him up, we intervened, and loaded the moribund animals into the trunk. Back home, we revived them, slowly, with heat lamps.

"Why do people do things like that?" my son asked quietly.

"Human beings are a sort of teeter-totter," I said, thinking about yin *and* yang. *"Some want to kill and the others want to save."*

"Us and them," he said solemnly.

"We and they," I nodded.

"I heard that some people kill deer because there are too many of them."

"Yes, but that's because the deer are starving and it is sometimes the right thing to do to stop suffering when you can."

"By killing?"

"It's a point of view," I answered.

"There are too many deer because we killed all the wolves that eat them," he said.

"Yes."

"Better if we didn't mess around with nature so much."

"I agree. When you get older, you can work to stop all that bad messing around."

"You were right, Dad."

"I was?"

He nodded. "Saving animals is even better than building a Lego."

It seems to me that a compassionate urge in the face of suffering is one of those innate human impulses I discussed at that breakfast years ago, and one that transcends philosophy. Compassion benefits all concerned.

My son is now training to be an astrobiologist.

. . .

There is good reason why trees are so venerated in Hinduism and other cultures. If there is one living thing on our planet worthy of worship, it is the tree. In many ways, trees are the most visible foundations of life on Earth. Absorbing nearly all their nutrition from the atmosphere, two trees provide oxygen for a family of four humans while simultaneously removing much of the carbon dioxide our industrial activities persist in pumping into the air. Trees almost never die of old age and are the source of pain-relieving, consciousness-expanding, resistant-strain-defeating, and even cancer-fighting medications. In our endless desire to amuse and distract ourselves with an ever-increasing range of material goods, we continue to plunder these perfect, egoless, natural apotheoses by plundering old-growth rainforests and temperate forests. Talk about losing love for the very nature that sustains us. Talk about shortsightedness. Even if framed in terms of how it benefits us—and please remember it's not all about us—razing these mature oxygen factories is, forgive the pun, a last-gasp maneuver. Even so, we continue to do it. Along the way, we also sacrifice indigenous languages and cultures we scarcely know, untold insects, animals, and plants. If there's anything we must stop right this moment, it is the logging and clearing of our planet's lungs—the temperate and tropical old-growth forests and jungles.

. . .

In the same way trillions of microorganisms comprise a human body, countless species of living creatures come together to make the superorganism we call Planet Earth. This superorganism depends upon a perfect population balance among its inhabitants the same way our body does. Planet Earth, the macroenvironment, has a limit to the number of human beings it can support, and we have exceeded that number. Depleting global energy reserves, destroying natural resources, producing ever-increasing levels of toxins and poisons, and outcompeting other species to the point they are extinguished, our species behaves just like a global cancer. Planet Earth fights back using genetic gender variations, fundamentalist religions, auto-immune diseases, and bacteria and viruses, all of which reduce our reproductive rate or kill us outright. We must gently, persistently, and compassionately persuade those who resist this reality to see it differently and thereby bring Earth back into balance. A start is to limit reproduction to a single child per family worldwide.

. . .

As we turn globally towards realizing the interconnectedness of all living things, why not consider not only how we live, but also what we do with our bodies after we die? We comment often about controversial real estate development and land use allocations, but far more rarely about the use of large tracts of land for cemeteries. More, the mainstream of our culture does not consider that both embalming and burying in thick or metal caskets makes the meat of us unavailable for recycling by microorganisms, scavengers, and opportunistic feeders. Why not return our dead bodies to the jungles, forests, and deserts, where they can contribute to the food chain as nature intended? Would this not be the holiest of holy ways to give back to that which has so long sustained us?

. . .

In the days before the population of human beings on earth reached such cancerous proportions, predator and prey existed in a fine and delicate balance. This balance had pervasive impact on the web of life, often engaging and affecting plants and animals not directly involved in each other's mortal dance. Aboriginal people understood these nuanced relationships and understood the consequences of overfishing or overhunting an area. They realized how many variables it took to make things just right, to create a world where human hunters and their progeny would be sustained. They understood the complex phenomena we now call "trophic cascades," in which a seemingly tiny change (overhunting a single species, for example) can have vast and unpredicted consequences. This understanding led to an appreciation for the wisdom and complexity of nature. It is a vanishingly rare occurrence to find a hunter today, living in an equally rare and remote locale, who is sensitive to this fine balance the way his forebears were. Such a hunter knows how to humanely and appropriately take game animals with his rifle and use the meat to survive. Recreational and trophy hunters, sadly, do not fall into this category, and must be kept from their cruel and self-indulgent games.

. . .

Bees and other pollinators are integral to the human food chain and are responsible for the survival of myriad of species of plants. As a side note, recent research suggests that bees learn while they sleep and may even dream. Destroying entire pollinator populations so as to preserve sales of particular pesticides, is like poking holes in the bottom of a ship so as to protect its sails. This is an egregious and outrageous example of shortsighted, human foolishness and greed. Ending the use of substances that kill pollinators is essential if we want to ensure our biological future. We can no longer afford any use whatsoever of bee-killing chemicals.

...

Planet Earth is not our playground to destroy. Despite the oft-cited, myths of the work of fiction known as the Judeo-Christian Bible, Earth was not given to human beings as a gift. The giver, a so-called god, is a fantasy and the giving never happened. Rather, our Earth is a large rock, bubbling hot on the inside, upon which life happened to appear due to an intersection of variables that may prove to be widespread, even common, across galaxies. Common or not, Earth is our home, and because of the power we have come to wield, it is increasingly imperative that we care for it with sensitivity and foresight. The more careful attention we pay to our world, the more we become aware not only of nature's complex and breathtaking beauty, but also of the sublime interconnectedness that is the hallmark of nature and the overarching characteristic of all that is.

Those who have most power and wealth
treat the planet as a thing to be possessed,
to be used and abused according to their own dictates.
But the planet is a living organism,
a Great Spiritual Integrity.

To violate this Integrity
is certain to call forth disaster
Since each and every one of us
is an inherent part of this very organism.

All attempts to control the world can only lead to its
decimation
and to our own demise
since we are an inseparable part of
of what we are senselessly trying to coerce.

Any attempt to possess the world
can only lead to its loss
and to our own dissolution
since we are an intrinsic part
of what we are foolishly trying to possess.

The world's pulse is our pulse.
The world's rhythms are our rhythms.
To treat our planet with care, moderation, and love
is to be in synchrony with ourselves
and to live in the Great Integrity.

—Laozi Stanza 29 ("We Are the World")[6]

---

6   Ralph Alan Dale, *Tao Te Ching*, London: Watkins 2016.

CHAPTER SIX

AWAKENING TO SPIRIT AND SERVICE

The great Daoist sage Zhuangzi conceives of four stages in the development of human consciousness. This system applies both to the individual person (considered within a single human's lifespan) and to the progression of humanity (considered against the backdrop of humanity's ongoing history). From my own point of view, these stages establish our place in space and time, as well as our evolutionary path. They are consequent to our biology, in particular to the architecture of our brain and its responses to threats regarding our survival. The stages reflect our answers to life-and-death situations, such as an onrushing predator or a deadly environmental drought, storm, or flood.

The first of these stages, which Zhuangzi sees as original and pure, is also infantile and undeveloped. Consciousness in this stage is, in a sense, *ideal*; however, in other ways, it remains merely nascent. The main characteristic here is its being perfectly non-dual—that is, is utterly one with our world. In this original conscious state, we don't see anything around us as any different from us. Existence is an experience rather than a thing, and it is a blurry existence, one not yet quite in focus.

In the next, second stage, we realize we are beings, alive and distinct from the world around us—both as individuals, and as humankind. We recognize objects around us, but we have not yet come into our habit of classifying or judging them or expressing our preferences. This stage of consciousness is a state of "I and other," but it is still an undifferentiated mishmash with a clear border but nothing else—no categories, groups, types, or other kind of classification.

The third stage in the advancement of consciousness involves classification. This is the stage where we begin to discern differences between things, places, people, and other sentient beings. It is in this stage where we notice how we react to things and how they react to us—as well as how we feel about the categories we have created. Like the previous two stages, this third stage is fluid. Our interaction with the world—our consciousness—reveals, shifts, turns, retreats, advances, and evolves. Our feelings about something we see, taste, hear, or smell may, for example, vary over the course of minutes or hours. This is the stage at which we begin to affix values to things, experience preferences, and become aware of the finiteness of resources, including the number of breaths and heartbeats we have left in our lives.

In the fourth and last stage in our progression, we find our consciousness migrating from a state of awareness and union with all things to an uncomfortable sense of alienation rife with anxiety and concern. This involves coveting things, people, positions, situations, and experiences, as well as fearing their loss and therefore grasping and clinging to them. This tightness, this closure of the fingers of the mind around the objects of our desire, creates what we call stress, a word that describes limited, narrow, and focused thinking—the very opposite of the state of relaxed navigation of the waters of life so vaunted by Daoist masters.

What can we do about this sad, downward spiral? Is the fourth stage of consciousness and its pernicious anxiety really inevitable and final? Or, if our progression towards stress can be reversed, do we really want to return to the first stage and its state of blurry infantilism? What of all the effort we have made to grow and self-actualize? Was it all for naught? What about the work we have done in and for the world, for those we love and those we will never meet? What about our anonymous philanthropy, our tireless, nameless, quiet, persistent, and steadfast efforts behind the scenes? Do we really have to throw it all away so as to become as supple of mind and limb as we were as yearlings?

The answer, thankfully, is no. The awakened mind in the Daoist tradition is a subtle and sophisticated one, a melding of adult experience and intelligence with the guilelessness, flexibility, genuine wonder, and uninhibitedness of childhood. Laozi portrays such a mind and person as a happy fool. To believe her to be foolish, depressed, disconnected, or giddy with stupidity is to miss Laozi's keen sense of irony. What he is really describing, as we can see at the end of this chapter, is someone who refuses to get sucked in to the petty nonsense of everyday life. This sage avoids being consumed by ordinary things, has a strong enough backbone and clear enough vision to keep her priorities straight, values peace and quiet, eschews trends, rises above common titillations, and cultivates *wuji* and the strength and wisdom that attend it.

In many ways, this Daoist ideal is the perfect subversive, the one who calls it the way she sees it and speaks out when others are either too afraid or too self-involved to do so. No wonder Daoists are revolutionary thinkers, architects of disruptive technologies and ideas, pillars of conscious communities, and occupiers of corner offices in companies where no one else has ever heard of the Eternal Mother, another term for *Dao*. No wonder we, Daoists, will go to any and all lengths to cultivate ourselves, no matter our personal challenges, and send the power of Daoist principles and ideas rippling outward into our communities and our world. Whether it is playing *tai chi ch'uan*, participating in a yoga class, building model ships, knitting, running, painting, listening to music (or making it), kayaking, volunteering in a museum, running thoughtful, ethical, compassionate enterprises, doing *pro bono* legal or healing work, or serving soup to homeless people, we must make sure to share our practices. Spirituality and service, it turns out, are inextricably interlinked.

RULES OF NATURE

Entropy is one of the most fundamental precepts of modern physics. It tells us that, since the Big Bang, the entire universe has been moving apart from its ultra-dense proto-core to a cold, motionless, diluted state of increasing chaos. It tells us that if we leave a house utterly alone for a hundred years, it will develop leaks, the paint will chip, dust will accumulate, the roof will cave in, the pipes will crack, and the floors will buckle. It tells us that the overarching tendency in the world is towards maximum disorder. Insofar as life is the only force we know of in the world that counters this fundamental trend, it is unique and wonderful—a marvel to behold. The guiding forces of life, biological laws, are approximately a fractal, which is to say they are more or less the same in design at every level of scale from the simplest viruses to the largest example of life we know, Planet Earth.

· · ·

It is time for the zero-sum competitive model of human society to come to an end. The planet is too small and we are too many to pit ourselves against each other for reasons of race, creed, heritage, or belief. Quantum physics and the new cosmology tell us that we are all made from atoms created at the time that the universe was born. We share these particles not only with other people we see in front of us right at this moment (and their great-great-grandparents), but with stars, birds, dinosaurs, water, bat dung, lizards, and bottle caps. Seen in this light, racism is just as objectionable as speciesism (thinking that people are in some cosmic way more important than crows), and patently more absurd.

. . .

Our belief systems and technology have moved us far from our biological roots. Every step we take away from those roots makes us more myopic, egotistic, and destructive. We must return to humility as a species, relinquish the flawed notion that we are unique in our use of tools and language, and abandon all notions of being superior to any other species. In general terms, we must replenish rather than destroy, nurture instead of criticize, heal not kill, plant not raze, cherish not violate, and focus on our sensitivity and awareness rather than our armaments and ambitions.

. . .

The notion of the human brain thriving within a glass container full of nutrient-rich fluid is a science-fiction fantasy. The brain needs the body. Indeed, through countless nerve cells too small to see, the complete brain is too deeply anatomically invested in the flesh to be inextricable from it. Mankind needs the earth as the brain needs the sinews, muscle, and bone of the body. So it is with the individual and society. Marooned alone on some far-off planet, the individual pines for company and dies. As we kill each other, so we kill ourselves; as we destroy our planet, so we guarantee our own demise.

BEYOND ORGANIZED RELIGION

Personal, mystical experiences are what legendary, religious leaders strove most keenly to share with us. Practicing tai chi or qigong and attentively listening to music are some of the ways we can attempt to recreate the mystical insights of our most important spiritual leaders. Such experiences cannot, however, be directly shared. To believe otherwise is to reduce the divine to the mundane. Mysticism is all-encompassing; organized religion is political and dogmatic. Dogma is rigid and unchanging; nature is flexible and ever-changing. Direct, mystical experience often catalyzes enlightenment; organized religion is more likely to generate exclusion, violence, and abuse. It's time to shed the credulous beliefs of our founding fathers, with their worship of falling stars, their narrow, easily-manipulated Puritan views. Why not eschew organized religion in favor of developing a direct connection with the world around us and a better understanding of the self? If we crave the community that organized religion offers, why not select a belief system that helps us move through our lives as water would, avoiding restraints, conflicts, and limitations, and freeing us from pernicious habits and aggressive behaviors?

...

Where aboriginal people concocted gods as a way to venerate nature, Western traditions invented gods to subdue it. Regardless of whether we grace their names with a capital letter (or forbid ourselves to speak their name at all), we love our fictitious gods so very much that we will duck our responsibilities in their names and even commit genocide to appease them. While some Eastern faiths also have pantheons of seductive concoctions, the violence and intolerance we derive from by being attached to them is largely absent, as is the notion that, no matter how much we transgress, our pet deities will wipe our slates clean. Let's remember, please, that gods live only between our ears. Let's stand strongly against those who insist otherwise and would force us to submit to their malignant fictions. The greatest teacher we have is the one that actually *exists*: that teacher is nature.

. . .

The number of indigenous, aboriginal cultures that have been destroyed by people who insisted upon foisting their beliefs on others is beyond count. The loss to humanity, from spiritual traditions and social know-how, to methods of sustainable agriculture, may never be known. What we can say for sure is that combining modern weaponry with the fantasies of those ancient novels, the Quran and Bible, the world is increasingly at risk of ending in a fireball.

. . .

Rivaling the best efforts of the Mongols and the Nazis, the self-serving propaganda of the Abrahamic faiths, empowered now by so-called marvels of technology, has sustained and intensified the horrors we perpetrate on each other—including genocide, jihadism, subjugation, and slavery. The latest wave of moral outrage arises from the mind virus of radical Islam, but it is only the latest wave, having been preceded by the Crusades, the Inquisition, and other not-so-charming expressions of Christian imperialism. Indeed, it could certainly be argued that a religion that promises those who blow up school buses full of innocent children a reward of tender, waiting virgins is no more malevolent than one that exhorts its

followers to precipitate nuclear Armageddon so as to hasten
the arrival of a savior and a refuge in an imagined paradise.

• • •

Humankind is in such a state of imbalance and disharmony
that freedom of religious expression threatens the survival of
our entire planet. Such freedom, while always desirable, may
no longer be the highest or most important good. We must
be able to clearly discern the difference between people and
ideology, between victims and the viruses of mind that infect
them. Any system of belief whose antiquated supernatural
tenets deny the rights of sentient beings to freely flourish must
be discarded. Violent proselytizing endangers world peace,
in much the same way as does discriminating against others
on the basis of age, gender, history, or race. Such dangerous
acts must be compassionately countered with education,
economic, and political sanctions, and, if absolutely necessary,
by military force.

• • •

Just as we have learned that the earth is not flat and there is
no white-bearded deity floating in the clouds telling us not to
pleasure ourselves in the bathroom stall, we have learned of the
senselessness of many of our cruel, destructive, anti-scientific
religious rituals. The merest whiff of the idea that someone
should be able to tell someone else about what they can do
to and with their own body should be enough to outrage any
conscious person. When we wage so-called "holy war," when
we set off a suicide bomb, picket a clinic, or deny someone
employment, we are operating at a subhuman moral level.
Religion can greatly benefit the individual and society, but only

if it is truly there for the benefit of the needy, cleaves to no intolerant or violent doctrine, and is a source of love, not hate.

. . .

The spiritual urge, that is the desire to connect with something larger than ourselves and discover a unifying force in the universe, is one of the most unique and beautiful characteristics of being human. Sadly, there are so very many who take advantage of spiritual hunger and pervert it for their own gain. Any religious figure who claims to occupy an interlocutor position between the human world and the divine is a person to avoid at all costs. Hucksterism seems to live in a stubborn human gene. Evolution should have eliminated it by now. The meme of "the chosen one," whether it applies to a religion, person, race, or any other human cohort, implies there is a chooser. This implication is not only delusional, it is offensive. It's one thing to select what flavor of ice cream we prefer; it's another thing altogether to elevate anyone for egoistic reasons. In the vast fabric of existence, all things rise to prominence at one point or another, only to subsequently decline. All things decline and eventually rise again. No judgments are being made on some dimensional or galactic scale. There need be no prejudices or separations in life, no specialness implied or expressed, especially regarding our own beliefs, heritage, or meager intelligence.

. . .

The river of religious exceptionalism is filled with bloated corpses and exudes the miasma of hate. Criticisms of war, genocide, and the flat-out silliness of cleaving to particular supernatural ideas are widespread, but we must address other, less well-trumpeted costs. These include the placing of limitations on education, the stifling of intellectual curiosity, the constraining of creativity, the planting of seeds of guilt and uncertainty in children, and the empowerment of antiquated and self-serving institutions that masquerade as something higher and better than the influence-peddling political flim-flams they really are. Included, too, in the dirt that must be swept out the door are barbaric mutilation rituals like male and female circumcisions, which must be completely outlawed without delay.

. . .

In 221 BCE, the ruler of the kingdom of Qin subjugated a bevy of kingdoms surrounding his own. At the conclusion of his bloody and merciless campaign, he installed himself as first emperor, Qin Shihuangdi, and the nation we now know as China was born. Shortly thereafter, Buddhism made its way across the Himalayas—by boat to the southern port at Guangzhou, too—and gained a foothold in Qin's new land. Initially a philosophy that offered a path out of personal suffering, the way of the Indian sage soon upended society by attacking the rigid social strata of Hindu society and by offering a way off the wheel of death and rebirth and into the Pure Land (the Buddhist version of Abrahamic heaven), by virtue of karma accumulated through good deeds. This new paradigm, attractive not only to low classes but to intellectuals as well, proved strong enough to transform Buddhism from the science of the mind Siddhartha Gautama originally intended into an organized faith.

Despite its indigenous, shamanic roots—or maybe because of them— Daoism lost ground to Buddhism. In much the same way that early Jews living under an elaborate and controlling code of laws were drawn to Christianity (with its reassuring doctrine of forgiveness and the unquestioned and unconditional love of Yahweh, a weather deity first associated, in Egyptian texts, with the nomadic Shasu of northern Arabia), Chinese increasingly chose Buddhism's beguiling promises over Daoism's rites and rituals.

In these tough times for Daoism, a scholar named Zhang Daoling rose to prominence. Zhang began reading Laozi's text when he was only ten years old. He ultimately became a scholar so formidable, he served as a professor at the Imperial Academy and thrice refused the Emperor Ming of the Han Dynasty's request that he serve as an imperial tutor. While simmering over about the degeneration of Daoism and, presumably, the rise of its rival from the west, Zhang visited a famous Daoist mountain. There, he was visited by a deified version of Laozi (elevating famous people to gods is a Chinese habit similar to canonization in the West), who revealed to Zhang some scriptures (a universal religious theme, it seems) and bestowed upon him the title of "Celestial Master." The story goes that Zhang, finding an immortal elixir in a sojourn to the mountains, chose to drink only half of it so as to be able to retain his mortal form. The consequence of his abstemiousness was the development of supernatural abilities. He is reputed to have been able to be in more than one place at a time, to fly, to command thunder and lightning, to walk among the stars, to cause mountains and seas to part before him (sounds familiar?), and to defeat the king of demons in combat.

Zhang went on to give Daoism a real makeover. He eliminated antiquated rituals like animal sacrifice and established, in Sichuan province, what would become one of the primary Daoist lineages. Devotees referred to it as the Celestial Master's School, while others gave it the name Five Pecks of Rice for the tax levied upon its adherents. Today, we would likely find Zhang a rule-giving scholar and formidable thinker who clearly had strong views about what people should and should not do. He was a wise man who understood that, by cultivating the self and helping others do the same, one can accomplish great things in the world. He taught meditation techniques that cured people mentally and physically and he was also a master *herbalist whose formulations healed the sick. He rose to great prominence because people loved his oratory, his ideas, and, most of all, his prescriptions.*

A key tenet of Daoism is that, in order to build the kind of mind that can support enlightenment, one needs a strong and healthy body. Zhang Daoling saw spiritual, physical, social, and political work as various aspects of the same thing. His prescriptions were so popular and successful that his organization solidified and spread, passing to his son, Zhang He, and then to his grandson, Zhang Lu. These two, and others, continued to give people what they wanted: health, something to believe in, and a cohort to which to belong. History has Zhang dying at the ripe old age of 123; legend, however, has him ascending to heaven in broad daylight while still being very much alive, the result of mastering arcane Daoist practices. In a larger sense, Zhang achieved immortality by understanding that the real role of religion is personal awakening and community service. He knew that, when it flows down to the lowest levels of society, an evolved religion floats all souls. Zhang is widely considered the father of religious Daoism, a belief system that is adhered to and followed by millions around the world to this day.

. . .

The latest Western religion, Scientism, suffers the same pitfalls as earlier ventures and is often a cover for authoritarianism. Unlike scientific inquiry itself, which is based on nature, cohered by a quorum, and constantly refined in the light of new ideas, evidence, and review, Scientism means the unquestioning placement of all things scientific above and beyond a moral framework. More, Scientism assumes science to be humankind's crowning purpose, trumping even art and love. In Scientism, superficiality outweighs depth, speed outweighs careful consideration, and rational thought undeservedly relegates intuition to the backburner of primitivism or superstition. Eschew Scientism in favor of science. Suspect the results of corporately-funded studies and of science being used in commerce. Scientism is, well, unscientific. Remember, the bedrock science of today is the crackpot science of yesteryear. Don't be too quick to dismiss apparent "crackpots." The pursuit of knowledge, indeed the act or state of knowing, while one of the consummate expressions of human experience, is not more important than acting with kindness and compassion toward all sentient beings.

IMPERMANENCE AND CHANGE

One year, I had pain in my knee, and went to see a doctor. He ordered an MRI and told me that the results suggested my knees were a war zone of inflammation. He asked me what I was doing to them; I said exercise, disinclined to share my admittedly overzealous Chinese kung fu regimen. He directed me to stop and I said that wasn't going to happen. He suggested some medication, and I said I tried to stay away from pharmaceuticals. He shrugged, told me surgery wasn't the answer, and that some people with this kind of problem had good luck with high doses of calcium. I bought some straight away, and after just twenty-four hours, noticed some improvement. Two days after that, the pain was gone.

I also noticed the taste of calcium precipitating into my saliva. Knowing that arterial plaque could involve calcium, I asked a number of medical folks, including my famous cardiologist father, if it was dangerous to take such supplements. Everyone assured me it was fine. I continued on the calcium for years until one morning, I woke with chest pain. Rushed to the hospital for emergency heart attack intervention, I was told that the most likely culprit was the calcium supplements. A few months later, the Food and Drug Administration issued a warning about mortality in men taking calcium supplements.

Complications arose after my initial crisis, including dangerous arrhythmias. Extreme measures were required, including strong medications and multiple surgeries. I was brought back from the mortal brink a couple of times, and it took me quite a while to recover from such a challenging cluster of events. After one of the surgeries, which not only failed but nearly killed me, I was so weak it took me the better part of ten minutes to climb a single flight of stairs. Exhausted, I stared longingly at my garden outside and at my tai chi straight sword propped against the wall. Unwilling to just lie around reading, but unable to do much more than that, I took the sword, went outside, and raised the blade until it touched a Japanese maple leaf that was dancing in a light breeze. Concentrating on feeling the force of the leaf on the blade, I practiced sensitivity and concentration until exhaustion overtook me and I returned to my sickbed. The next day, I got up and did the same thing again, this time using my other hand.

Some months into my rehabilitation, my tai chi master came to visit from Guangzhou. We met in the park for a tai chi lesson, and I could see he was shocked by my condition. The last time he'd seen me I'd been robust, strong, energetic, and reasonably skillful. Sadly, I had become a shadow of my former self. I moved like a hundred-year-old man, lacked stamina, and appeared largely bereft of my previous flexibility and power. Watching his face, I saw him war with his emotions over my decline.

"I have an idea for you," he said. "Did you happen to bring a straight sword?"

A few minutes later, we were standing beneath a Florida oak tree. "Raise your blade and touch a leaf," he directed. "Notice how the wind

*moves it. See if you can feel the pressure from the wind on the leaf.
See if you can follow it without losing contact. This is a wonderful
exercise for sensitivity."*

*I performed the exercise with him for half an hour or so. I didn't have
the heart to tell him I'd already figured it out on my own. Later, when
we were leaving the park, he told me he was proud of me. He is not
a warm and fuzzy type and had never said anything like that to me
before. I found myself choked up.*

*"When something like this happens to most guys, their practice is
over," he said. "They just retire to the beach in Mexico and drink beer
until they die."*

"I'm not that kind of guy," I said.

*"That's why I'm proud of you. Anyway, what happened is very
good for you."*

*His words stunned me. If it had been anyone else, I might have
exploded in a description of the pain and suffering my family
and I had endured as the result of my troubles. Instead, because I
loved and respected my teacher so much, I took a deep breath. "You
think?" I said.*

*He nodded. "Martial arts are about beating an opponent. The most
powerful opponent you can ever have is death. You've seen him.
You've beaten him. In the end, he will win, but, when he comes for the
last time he will be familiar and you won't be afraid. Because of this,
you have nothing to prove anymore, not to yourself or anyone else."*

"I didn't like him much," I said.

*He nodded. "There's another thing. Before, you relied on your strength
to do everything, and your mind was fast and clear. Now, because
you are weak and everything comes slowly to you, you have to find*

another way to develop. You have to relax. You have to learn how to follow the way of nature, how to sense small forces, how to read an opponent's energy and intention. It will be difficult but, in a year or so, you will improve as much as if you'd spent another twenty-five years practicing."

We, Daoists, have a phrase. "The Dao is big." The idea is to always try and have the broadest perspective. To think of our attention as a camera with a zoom lens. Trapped in the heat of the moment, the lens is in macro mode. All we can see is the tiny, yellow edge in the middle of the frame. Dialed back a click or two, we see a beautiful flower. Dialed back even further, we see a field of beautiful flowers. Zoomed out some more, we see a lovely countryside. Continuing our exercise, we eventually float in space, looking down at our beautiful blue planet. Doing this is a meditation, a game, as whatever is bothering us loses immediacy, loses importance, and fades away until it is no more than a speck in the big picture.

Thinking about it, I realized I would have preferred the additional quarter-century of practice my master mentioned to the misery I had endured. Of course, I did not have the choice. Lessons on the path to self-actualization are unpredictable and can be rough. Still, if we persevere, the rewards come to us and to the world around us.

• • •

The human mind is free to recognize that reality is a system, not a snapshot. Despite our imaginary devils and gods (devices to represent the twin poles of our characters), it is actually we, humans, who are defined by being both good and evil, impulsive and patient, scheming and credulous, happy and sad, angry and joyful, generous and stingy, considerate and callous, deceptive and honest, and so much more. Understanding that our inner landscape will constantly shift, recognizing this to be a human characteristic, not a defect (and the source of our creativity) makes it easier to nudge ourselves in the direction we really want to go.

· · ·

When we frame objects, people, or events as being either good or bad, we forget the limitations of our points of view—and just how quickly the facts of a situation can change. There are many Daoist stories that chronicle how shifting circumstances turn a calamity into a blessing. Missed airline flights crash. Lost jobs make way for better opportunities. Failed relationships prepare us for more helpful ones. When we are tempted to feel that our day, or even our entire life, could not get any worse, the cosmic pendulum has a way of suddenly reversing direction and showing us how wrong we were, revealing all the opportunities and benefits of a long, down period, or simply a lousy day. Take heart. Reversal is nigh. It is the nature of cycles and cycles are the nature of *Dao*. We might wish to meditate upon this.

· · ·

Obstacles can be great blessings and great learning opportunities. So can conflicts. If Door #1 means using force against force, and Door #2 means letting someone walk all over you, then the best solution to life's disagreements is Door #3, a solution unique to the situational specifics. Meditation and introspection can help us achieve the kind of detached, equanimous, spontaneous, and creative mind that easily provides us with such a special resolution to conflict. Please spread the word that the symbol for this thinking is to raise the left hand and hold the three middle fingers upright, pinkie and thumb tucked together, palm forward.

. . .

Failure and loss are features of living and features of dying, too. When we suffer either, our frustration and pain turn the zoom lens of our life to maximum magnification, reducing the world to only our pain. Through meditation or visualization techniques, we can see the world around us a bit more clearly, see the people who wish us well, who are there for us, the gifts we have given, and those we have received. We see the context of our lives in terms of past and future and understand we are more beings of time than we are beings of space. Our lives are mere flickers of energy on a wet rock floating in the vastness of space. From this perspective, we are free to recognize that our troubles are of no real significance. Thence we can find it easy for us to let go, regain optimism, and feel recharged and ready to repair our wounds and try again. The universe is much bigger than we think it is.

. . .

Compassionate impulses are straightforward and to be prized; compassionate actions, however, are a more complicated proposition. Sometimes, the right thing to do—feed the hungry, heal the sick, clean the stream, and protect the weak— is obvious. Sometimes, however, knowing what to do requires both a long term perspective and a societal/cultural context. When in doubt, we are better off asking and conferring than acting rashly. In this way, we avoid doing more harm than good.

. . .

It is entirely possible that we are wrong about the nature of life and death. Rather than the inevitable end of everything dear, death may in fact signal a return to the state of transcendent belonging we all crave deep down. Every one of us will discover the truth about this soon enough. In the meantime, rather than living for the rewards of an afterlife promised to us by people (not gods) who don't know what lies ahead any better than we do, why not treasure each day, each moment, right now? Cherish the process of living. Honor the opportunities for experience, service, and growth, that life provides. Let's give focused attention, energy, and purpose to the life we are living today while remaining open to the idea that death may open the door to something even more marvelous at some future time.

...

We spend much of our lives in an effort to translate external activities into neurotransmitters. Circumstances, achievements, and even relationships are all about brain chemistry. We're not really after fancy things; we're after how they make us feel. We're not really after that big job; we're after the feeling of power that comes with it. We're not really after a relationship's social status or some material gain it may bring us; we want to love and be loved. It's all about avoiding pain and finding pleasure. The virtual world can provide that pleasure, but only on a temporary basis. The game we play ceases to be challenging and rewarding until we "level up." If we play long enough, we run out of levels. In the case of street drugs, hitting the limit of such substances can cost us our lives. The most profound neuro-cocktails, however, are not simply those that bring us pleasure but those that give us a sense of self-worth. Going beyond peak experiences to find out who and what we are, and to discover our place in the world, is, in the end, the master game.

TRANSCENDENCE

Sixty-six million years ago, an asteroid three kilometers across splashed down with speed and force into the shallow waters off the Yucatán Peninsula. The water was vaporized and the sediment below was forced into the atmosphere as a giant cloud of dust. If a mere half a minute had passed before impact, the rotation of the Earth and the angle of entry would have put the hot, fast rock from space deep into the ocean where it would have raised steam, not dust. Without the dust, the sun would not have been blocked, and plants would not have died out. If plants had not died out, the dinosaurs would not have starved. If the dinosaurs had not starved, there would been no room for the rise of the mammals. If the mammals had not risen, human beings would not exist. It was not a god, but rather a bit of extra-terrestrial serendipity working through evolution that led to monkeys writing and reading books like this one. Isn't it time for an evolutionary leap of spirit, one that imbues us all with a sudden clarity about how inappropriate the old ways have become, how important it is we help each other, and how critical it is that we become not destroyers of the world but its stewards? Without this evolutionary release of the talents lying dormant in our minds, humankind and most other species on Earth are doomed.

. . .

The dawn of artificial intelligence notwithstanding, human mind makes its greatest discoveries through flashes of insight that arise from mental housecleaning. Humanity's collective understanding of the world is growing at such a rate that a huge percentage of the "facts" we learn in school and on the job will become obsolete in just a few years. The sage, after years of study, translation, integration, reading, writing, and calculating, eventually reaches the place where she lets all that go, empties her library, takes a deep breath, and looks at the world with eyes trained but now freed to see things far more clearly, far more deeply.

The difference between a formal "yes"
and a casual "yeah"—how slight!
The difference between knowing the Truth
and not knowing it—how great!

Must I fear what others fear?
Should I fear desolation
when there is abundance?
Should I fear darkness
when that light is shining everywhere?
Nonsense!
The people of this world are steeped in their merrymaking
as if gorging at a great feast
or watching the sights of springtime
Yet here I sit, without a sign,
staring blank-eyed like a child

I am but a guest in this world
While others rush about to get things done
I accept what is offered
Oh, my mind is like that of a fool
aloof to the clamor of life around me
Everyone seems so bright and alive
with the sharp distinctions of the day
I appear dark and dull
with the blending of differences by night

I am drifting like an ocean, floating like the high winds
Everyone is so rooted in this world
yet I have no place to rest my head
Indeed I am different...
I have no treasure but the Eternal Mother
I have no food but what comes from her breast

—Laozi Stanza 20[7]

---

7   Jonathan Star, *Tao Te Ching—The Definitive Edition*, New York: Jeremy P. Tarcher/Putnam, 2001.

The most fundamental spiritual experience is the realization that something is happening. What is that something? The moment we ask that question, we have veered off the track of questing and into the honey trap of analysis. It's fun to organize, categorize, prioritize, alphabetize, and memorize, yet none of those exercises really gets us any closer to Knowing. The immanent sense of progression, movement, and unfolding in the world (all these words are somehow inadequate), fills all true seekers with a sense of awe and wonder.

. . .

Do not let anyone judge your spiritual experiences by subjecting them to rational, logical, and scientific analysis. We must seek *inner*standing—both in the sense of a deeper clarity about the world inside us and in the sense of self-respect— instead of understanding. If someone tells us our experience is just the result of some neurotransmitter cocktail, self-delusion, or wishful thinking, simply remind them that if someone had told us a hundred years ago that matter was an illusion, that even the tiniest of particles that comprise our universe have no substance at all but are, instead, mathematical probability functions that can be smashed together hard and fast in such a way as to blow up a city, we would have had them locked up in the loony bin. Now we have supercolliders, quantum mechanics, and, sadly, hydrogen bombs. Let's believe in the reality of our inner experience, but let's not apply intellect to it. Let's recognize that there is something else out there, something far deeper and more complex. Let's remember, please, that there is nothing so shallow as human intelligence.

. . .

I was out riding my bike recently, when it occurred to me that I had been singularly lucky to not experience any flat tires lately. In fact, I'd had the bicycle for a year, and hadn't done a thing to it, hadn't even adjusted the seat, brakes, or cables. This is in stark contrast to the last bike I'd had, which seemed to pop a tube every other ride.

No sooner had my good fortune on the ride occurred to me, when I heard a muffled puff, felt the handlebars wiggle, and the ride turned rough. I hopped off the bike and set about replacing the tube on the rear tire, which was flat as an asphalt runway. I found no cause for the blow-out—no thorn, no rough spoke-head, no failure at the valve, nothing obvious. I got the job done, got back on the bike, and rode for about another mile before I heard another, slightly louder puff while in a hard, fast corner. I nearly lost control of the bike as the front tube also let go. I didn't have a second spare with me, so I walked the bike home and repaired it there.

I assumed I would find the same kind of inner tube as I'd found in the front and figured I was merely the victim of a bad manufacturing batch. The second tube, though, was of a different brand entirely. Again, I discovered no obvious reason for the tube failure—no nail, no bad valve, no protruding spoke, nothing. I knew I had not overinflated the tubes, as I am always careful with the tire gauge. I checked the sidewalls of both tires with a magnifying glass, figuring that my aging eyes had missed something. Again, I could find no reason for the problem. Then, I remembered congratulating myself on a blow-out-free ride just moments before the first tube failure. Fleetingly, I wondered whether my thoughts had in some way perversely materialized the incident—whether, in fact, there was any relationship between my thoughts and the material world, whether the trendy concept of "manifesting" so popular in New Age doctrine, might possibly be real.

Years ago, I had a cheap little convertible. Small and sporty, foreign and cute, it provided me countless miles of top-down driving enjoyment. I loved that little car and it seemed to love me back, being reliable despite having an unreliable reputation and never causing me a lick of trouble. After driving it for a number of years, I became fixated on a newer model. I grew dissatisfied with the lackluster acceleration of my old drop-top, and uncomfortable with its notchy transmission, hard seats, lousy radio, and the way it pitched sideways when going through corners.

Suddenly, as if I had raised some kind of automotive orchestral baton and signaled the start of a disastrous melody, my little car began to fall apart. The window cranks broke off, the transmission stuck, the engine revved with great reluctance, the starter motor gave out, the chassis began to creak, and the suspension took to groaning over bumps. The canvas top sprung leaks and blue smoke began to pour from the tailpipe. Within a matter of weeks of losing my favor, it cost me more than it was worth to repair. I sold it a short time later.

As it was disintegrating, I could not help wondering why. Sure, the changes in the car were objectively true, but was I so tuned-in to my little ride that I became subconsciously aware of its degradation before I consciously recognized it? Was any causation purely in my head, or did the car somehow "know" I didn't care about it anymore and willed itself to "die?" Correspondingly, had my prior, long term positive feelings somehow lent a cohering force to the thing, contributing to its reliability and longevity? I know the word "logic" might be a stretch in this context—indeed, there is no commonly accepted mechanism to explain how we feel about inanimate objects can affect them—but maybe there is more to this question than meets the eye. Discoveries in quantum mechanics suggest a universe far more nuanced and complex than the Newtonian one existing in the worldview that most of us hold, a world in which ideas and emotions hold sway outside of the electrical impulses and chemicals in our brain.

Experience, instinct, and reason all tell me that there is in fact a relationship between our attitudes and the world around us. Books continue to be written about the power of our intentions to manifest results, particularly in our relationships with others. Nobody doubts that the exquisite, invisible, and emotional antennae borne by the people around us allow them to react and respond to the "vibe" we put off. No pet owner doubts that his dog, cat, bird, or snake can respond to her moods. So far, we haven't come to accept that we can change inanimate objects with our attitudes and emotions, but perhaps that will change, too.

Before the dawn of the New Physics, people who saw the world this way were branded crackpots, mystics, witches, hippies, or fools. It is very likely the same was said about those who denied that the world was flat. If a century ago one had suggested that the world was comprised of invisible particles so tiny a zillion of them could dance on the head of a pin, one would have been deemed quite mad. If one advanced the further proposition that smashing two of those particles would create a chain reaction strong enough to level New York City, one would have been put in chains and carted off to a mental ward. Today, in the age of Dark Matter and Dark Energy, when matter is acknowledged to be illusory and everything seen as vibration and probability, when we have confirmed the existence of a God Particle and gravitational waves, it no longer seems so farfetched to imagine that our thoughts and feelings might affect the delicate and complex function of that collection of parts, electricity, and processes we call a "car."

It may be that spiritual awakening involves reframing the way we view the world. It may be that enlightenment is not as much about learning new ideas as it is about removing filters unwittingly installed by prejudice and ignorance. It may very well be that our minds can affect not only our relationships but also our phones, our toasters, our intercontinental ballistic missiles, and everything in between.

Awakening the ability to sense and correlate our intention with results in the inanimate world might lead to greater understanding of how things really work.

Such a deeper understanding, of course, is what Daoists have always been after.

. . .

Ancient thinkers were not distracted by digital or virtual worlds, nor by the speed-and-greed frenzy of modern life. They had the same fine brains we do, but were able to indulge in decades of solitary observation in order to formulate an understanding of the workings of the natural world. That individual experience at the frontier of reality has largely been replaced by the scientific method, which aggregates the thoughts and insights of several millennia worth of observers into a new coherent synthesis. This method is rich, marvelous, powerful, and also incomplete and unbalanced. Evidence for its benefits is everywhere; evidence for its shortcomings are as well, primarily in the devastation caused by technology. Daoism teaches us that it is the very act of individually paying attention to nature, not learning about it through the work of others, that offers the spiritual payoff. Thus, rather than seeing only the Old Way and the New Way, and demonizing one or the other, why not look for a Door #3 in this arena, where we recognize that we still lack the tools for a complete understanding of nature, and may always lack them? Why not recognize that spiritual or metaphysical experiences of reincarnation, entities and energies, dreams and premonitions, and multiple realities may be explainable by both features of our neurological wiring *and* by levels of existence that both evolution and culture filter out? Let's keep our minds open. Let's use all the tools at our disposal. Let's use the full range of our senses and faculties at all times. Let's drop judgment, be present, and see what happens when we allow things we often dismiss to turn out to be true.

. . .

The word "meditation" refers to a wide range of activities in the same way the word "hobbies" refers to a wide range of interests and pastimes and the word "sports" refers to the games we play and the thrills we seek. What is interesting about the various types of meditation, especially within the context of spirit and service, is that certain versions can actually deliver on the promises religions make. Specifically, meditation can offer emotional succor in hard times, cultivate a sense of gratitude that allows us to live life more deeply, and give us a transcendent sense of belonging to something larger than ourselves. If there is a religion or philosophy that makes sense in the age of science and reason, one that is congruent with our evolution as compassionate and awake beings, it is Daoism and its meditative practices.

. . .

Tai chi was once a battlefield art and, as such, included techniques and training in many traditional Chinese weapons. These included maces, iron rods called "sword breakers," spears, axes, halberds, and swords. Most of the swords had curves. One, however, was straight, making it essentially a long, double-edged dagger designed for thrusting and piercing attacks.

Tradition refers to this straight sword as the heart of Chinese kung fu (tai chi is a style of kung fu), because of its long and exalted tradition and because the demands of its use put it into the hands of the most skilled warriors. To wield this weapon well, one must have a quiet mind, agile body, good reflexes, and dexterous wrists. I often tell students who are ambivalent about employing weapons in their practice that the modern-day use of the sword is to spiritually slice through the chains that keep us from growing and bisect the ropes that bind us to habits and beliefs no longer of service.

There are few sequences of movements in any of the world's combat or dance styles that are more elegant, intricate, relaxed, and flat-out inspiring than those of the traditional Chen Style tai chi straight sword. These movements entail thrusting, slicing, chopping, parrying and blocking, all the while being sensitive, seeking, sticking, lively, and soft. The traditional sword sequence is one of traditional Chinese culture's great treasures and learning it is one of life's great pleasures, too.

Many movements in the form bear poetic names. Some evoke animals, such as Green Dragon Rises from Water, Boa Whips Around, Swallow Pecks Mud, White Ape Offers Fruit, *or* Black Bear Turns Around. *Others pay homage to figures in Chinese mythology, like* Zhong Kui Holds His Sword *or* Nezha Searches the Sea. *Some moves, however, bear pedestrian monikers. My beloved master was suffering through watching my beginner's take on one of these,* Stab Upward, *decades ago in a South Florida park. The rising sun danced on the surface of a lake nearby and a light breeze rustled the leaves of an encircling stand of live oaks. A beautiful Giant Swallowtail butterfly fluttered around me. I froze in place, watching, arms stretched high, as it touched down on the very tip of my blade.*

It was a special moment. The vibrant, natural beauty of the scene, the butterfly's black-and-yellow wings spread against the gathering blue of the morning sky, the stillness of my concentrating mind, and the connection I imagined to all the people across the world and across time who had practiced this same move, all left me with an upwelling of emotion.

"What does this mean?" I asked my master.

"What does what mean?"

Unwilling to break the magic by taking a hand off the sword to point, I gestured at the butterfly with my chin. "The butterfly. Is it an auspicious sign in Chinese martial lore?"

He blinked at me. "Auspicious how?"

"You tell me. I mean the way he chose just this moment to perch on my sword."

He shook his head and laughed. "You, artists. Always trying to make something more than what is. Isn't it enough that the day is beautiful, your practice is getting better, and we have time to spend together before I have to go back to China? Isn't it enough that you see this marvel of nature up close? Why do we have to add anything to all that? The butterfly landed on your sword because it was tired and needed to rest. The trees were too high and the ground was too low!"

I've thought about this little story for years. On the surface, it makes me look a rube, an occupational hazard for a klutzy Westerner trying to learn Chinese kung fu. The story, though, sheds light on a lot more than my own silliness, revealing as it does how woefully most of us underappreciate nature, the marvel of life itself, and the sublime complexity and beauty of each and every moment. Too, it highlights how we are all so willing to ignore the practical in favor of the imaginary and disregard reality in favor of the stories we tell ourselves.

Enjoying the beauty of nature and culture is one of life's most singular and wonderful aspects. Imbuing things with more significance than they have is less likely than missing that very significance in the hustle and bustle of everyday life. My teacher was right in his comment. The answer to my question was there all along. We don't have to search for the wonder. If we simply pay attention, we can always find something divine, mystical, and mysterious in the world—a child's laugh, a lover's look, the grasp of a praying mantis, the scent of an orange grove, the beauty of a sunrise, the tug of a full moon, or the song of a nightingale.

All of it is there all the time.

AFTERWORD

Most people think a monk's life must take place in a monastery, that it requires celibacy, and is filled with constant ritual and prayer. While that description applies to many monks, particularly in the Buddhist tradition, there are others out in the world living different lifestyles and finding different ways to make a contribution and be of service. The Dalai Lama became a leader and a politician. Gregor Mendel became the father of modern genetics. Takuan Soho, the Zen Buddhist author and monk, served as advisor to Japan's most famous swordsmen as well as the shogun, and was enough of a gourmet to have Japanese pickles named after him. Gregoryi Rasputin, faith-healing mystic and confidant of the Russian royal family, influenced the course of World War I and the 1917 fall of the Russian Empire. Thích Nhát Hanh, peace activist and New Age teacher, reaches countless eager ears and eyes with his lectures and books. Martin Luther reformed a religion and Siddhartha Gautama (aka the Buddha) founded one. Matthieu Ricard, known as "the world's happiest man," is, among other things, an author, teacher, and activist for animal rights and veganism. Benedict of Nursia became the patron saint of Europe. In my own far, far more modest role, I have the high privilege of sharing Daoist ideas with the Western world.

It is, therefore, my heartfelt hope that readers take away from this manifesto an appreciation of the *yin* and *yang* of choices and beliefs. On the one hand, we are often slaves to culture, society, traditions, family history, and our own personal experience. On the other hand, we are free to learn, grow, and shed our assumptions, drop our prejudices, and withhold our judgments. This is a characteristic not only of human beings but of all conscious creatures. Plants, though flattened by bulldozers, crack through concrete in their quest for light. Turtles learn their way through mazes after many frustrating attempts. Abused, vicious dogs can be rehabilitated in loving homes, and rogue elephants, angry at villagers who have slaughtered their families, can be set free in new habitats to form fresh, nurturing relationships.

Fears are the chains that bind us; ideas are the keys that set us free. All the concepts, suggestions, exhortations, and admonitions in this book have as their sole *raison d'être* the creation of a world absent of damage and limitations, a utopian home to all sentient beings, and even an intergalactic beacon sending the message to aliens inhabiting other planets or dimensions, "Hey, look at us, look how great we have become, look what consciousness can bring and do."

Perhaps, someday, such beings will visit and find us to be all that we have always wanted to be: kindly stewards of our home and fearless adventurers, not only in the realm of technology but at the farthest limits of our potential. Until then, please spread the word about this manifesto. Exhort others to buy it, borrow it, download it, and give it life. Discuss the ideas it contains as I proposed in the introduction, argue about them (hopefully *for* them), and use the energy between these covers to encourage evolution and revolution in the direction of a better you and a better world. Without leading to action, all these words are for naught.

Nine bows for your kind attention. If you feel moved to join me in my quest to spread Daoist ideas, please check out www. monkyunrou.com.

I dreamed I saw Joe Hill last night,
Alive as you and me.
Says I, "But Joe, you're ten years dead—"
"I never died," says he.
"I never died," says he.

"The copper bosses killed you, Joe,"
"They shot you, Joe!" says I—
"Takes more than guns to kill a man,"
Says Joe, "I didn't die,"
Says Joe, "I didn't die."

And standing there, as big as life,
And smiling with his eyes—
Says Joe, "What they can never kill,"
"Went on to organize,"
"Went on to organize."

From San Diego up to Maine,
In every mine and mill,
Where working folks defend their rights,
It's there you find Joe Hill,
It's there you find Joe Hill.

I dreamed I saw Joe Hill last night,
Alive as you and me.
Says I "But Joe, you're ten years dead—"
"I never died," says he.
"I never died." says he.

—Joan Baez, "Joe Hill"

ACKNOWLEDGMENTS

Deepest and most profound thanks to my teacher and friend Master Max Yan. Meeting you not only changed my life but gave it purpose and direction. I will forever be grateful. Nine bows to Master Pan Chongxian for ordination and support and to Master Che Gaofei for friendship and lessons. A hug and kiss to my dear wife, staunchest supporter, and literary agent, Janelle Schindler. These words would still be gathering dust in a drawer without your efforts, and I'd likely be floating around on a cloud somewhere with no clear sense of the ground.

Thanks to my kung fu brother Todd Plager for his ready ear and sage counsel. Thanks to my indoor students, Jennifer Beimel, Joshua Berkowitz, Dolph Brust, Grant Clyman, Rodney Cohen, Christopher Dankowski, Jose Fraga, Michael Goldman, E. Scott Leaderman, Nelson Reyes, William Simmons, and Dan Zhou for your hard work, loyalty, feedback, teaching assistance, and for keeping me in line with a whistle, a cough, and sometimes a needed dose of deprecating humor. Thanks to the tai chi poster girl, Debbie Zinna, for inspiring all of us, and to Jasmin Moreno for proving that the right kid can change her life with tai chi. Thanks to Alexa Dysch for some solid proofreading, to my editors, Brenda Knight and MJ Fievre, to Roberto Núñez for his beautiful layout and to all the rest of the folks at Mango Publishing for making this book a reality.

MONK YUN ROU

Yun Rou, whose name means "Soft Cloud," received his academic training at Yale, Cornell, and the University of California. A long-time practitioner of Daoist arts in the *Shangqing* tradition, he was ordained a Taoist monk in the *Quanzhen* sect of Daoism at the Pure Yang Temple in Guangzhou, China and now teaches Daoist arts in South Florida and worldwide. After a few crime novels and a brief stint in Hollywood, his writings and teachings now propagate Taoist themes, mythologies, and prescriptions.

CPSIA information can be obtained
at www.ICGtesting.com
Printed in the USA
JSHW020916101221
21161JS00003B/3